"雅思9分真题库"丛书

雅思9分真题库
——听力密题及解析

启德考培产品中心　编著

电子工业出版社·

Publishing House of Electronics Industry

北京·BEIJING

图书在版编目(CIP)数据

雅思9分真题库. 听力密题及解析 / 启德考培产品中心编著. —北京：电子工业出版社，2023.9

ISBN 978-7-121-46341-9

Ⅰ．①雅…　Ⅱ．①启…　Ⅲ．①IELTS－听说教学－自学参考资料　Ⅳ．①H310.41

中国国家版本馆CIP数据核字（2023）第175460号

雅思9分真题库——听力密题及解析

启德考培产品中心　编著

责任编辑： 王昭松

印　　刷： 北京市大天乐投资管理有限公司

装　　订： 北京市大天乐投资管理有限公司

出版发行： 电子工业出版社

北京市海淀区万寿路173信箱　　邮编：100036

开　　本： 787×1 092　1/16　**印张：** 15　**字数：** 499.2千字

版　　次： 2023 年 9 月第 1 版

印　　次： 2023 年 9 月第 1 次印刷

印　　数： 3 000 册　**定价：** 59.00 元

凡所购买电子工业出版社图书有缺损问题，请向购买书店调换。若书店售缺，请与本社发行部联系，联系及邮购电话：（010）88254888，88258888。

质量投诉请发邮件至zlts@phei.com.cn，盗版侵权举报请发邮件至dbqq@phei.com.cn。

本书咨询联系方式：（010）88254015，wangzs@phei.com.cn。

《雅思9分真题库——听力密题及解析》编委会

主　编：郑庆利

编　委：（按姓氏笔画排序）

牛佳乐乐　石金娥　刘　苏

杨　帆　张　萌　其格乐罕　俞　丹

郭星彤　高璨然　曹　彧　Michael Tai

前言 | PREFACE

随着全球新冠疫情的逐渐缓解，我们迎来了一个新的时代，一个恢复和振兴的时代。国际教育与留学行业不断回暖，留学申请人数不断回升，对雅思考试的需求也随之反弹。顺应这一趋势，我们精心打造了"雅思9分真题库"这套备考丛书，旨在帮助各位考生顺利通过雅思考试，被心仪的学校录取。

雅思考试是每一位想要出国留学的学生需要闯过的语言关。无论是计划攻读学士、硕士研究生还是博士研究生学位，雅思成绩都是迈向梦想之门的第一步。"雅思9分真题库"丛书包含听、说、读、写四本书，以还原真题为主，提供大量切实可用的表达素材和解题思路，帮助考生全面提升各项技能，使备考更加系统和有针对性。我们对考生备考的压力和难处感同身受，在书中总结了诸多备考攻略和技巧，帮助考生合理规划备考时间、提高答题速度、增强口语和写作表达能力。

听力和阅读部分各包含六套历年雅思考试还原真题。这些题目都是经过精心挑选的最具代表性的题目，还原度非常高。每一篇文章或听力材料后面都非常详细地总结了相关的核心词汇，更重要的是，我们对每一道题都进行了非常详尽的解析，包括各类题型的解题技巧、如何定位、如何分析选项等，帮助考生更好地理解题目要求和掌握解题思路。我们深知，掌握好解题技巧是备考的关键，因此我们特别注重解析部分的详细性和清晰度。阅读部分还精选了一些长难句进行讲解，这些句子中的词汇、句式结构和语法点不但能帮助考生更好地理解阅读文章，也可以助力写作。

写作和口语部分以话题为基础，为考生准备了大量高扩展性、高实用性、地道的表达和素材及通用的答题结构，让考生高效备考。口语部分为相关素材提供了图片，便于联想和记忆。写作部分独创"雅思写作母题方法论"，揭露雅思写作"套路"。书中讨论的话题均经过精心整理，覆盖绝大多数的雅思口语和写作题目。从词汇到句子，从逻辑结构到范文解析，解决雅思口语和写作备考中无话可说、不会组织语言的问题。

然而，"雅思9分真题库"丛书并非仅是

书中的内容。我们深知在备考过程中刷题的重要性，通过大量的练习，考生可以熟悉考试形式、掌握解题技巧，储备有用的素材，从而更好地应对考试。为此，我们在启德考培在线网站（https://online.eickaopei.com）特别推出了6套真题。这些真题均模拟了真实的考试场景，通过这些真题，考生将有机会进行更多的练习，巩固和扩展知识，全面提高备考水平。我们自主研发的"启德 i 备考"小程序不但有最新的雅思口语和写作题目，还有由母语为英语的外教撰写的范文。此外，我们还特别推出了口语音频，考生可以在这一平台上直接进行口语练习，解决口语不知道怎么练和练了无从知道效果的问题，这将大大提高考生的口语表达能力，为考生在口语考试中取得优异成绩提供有力支持。

最后，感谢产品中心每一位成员的辛苦付出。他们的专业素养和无私奉献是本套丛书成功出版的重要保证。他们在题目挑选和内容组织等方面投入了大量心血，力求将最优质的内容呈现给广大考生。我们衷心希望"雅思 9 分真题库"丛书能够成为考生攻克雅思考试的一把利剑，实现自己的留学梦想。

祝愿各位考生都能在雅思考试中取得优异成绩，开启崭新的留学之旅！

启德教育集团考培产品中心

★ 本书使用指南

1. 完成题目

请在播放录音时按照实际考试时间要求完成题目。

2. 核对答案

根据书中提供的参考答案核对自己的答案，记录每部分的正确题数，以便评测学习效果。

3. 反思错题

对于答错的题目，根据书中提供的解析分析原因。可能的原因包括生词障碍、预判错误、抓不住关键词等。通过剖析错误的原因，明确自己的提升方向。

4. 整理生词和同义替换词

整理题目、录音文本与参考答案中的生词和同义替换词并记忆。

5. 精听文本

对照录音文本逐句精听，理解每句话的含义并进行复述。

6. 模考练习

保留两套试卷在考前一个月进行模考，严格模拟真实的考试时间与流程，用于评估自己目前的听力水平。

通过反复练习和不断改进，相信本书可以帮助各位考生更好地应对雅思听力考试，提高听力技能，取得理想的目标分数！

目录 CONTENTS

Section 1 雅思听力真题还原

Section 2　雅思听力逐题精讲解析

Section 3　录音文本

Section 4　参考答案

01

Section 1

雅思听力真题
还原

Test 1

Listening test audio

Part 1   *Questions 1-10*

Complete the notes below.

*Write **NO MORE THAN TWO WORDS AND/OR A NUMBER** for each answer.*

Amateur Dramatic Association

Assistant name: Jane (example)

Mailing address: 117/155 Green Street

Rehearsal address: the **1**............... House

Requirements

● No experience required, but especially want actors and **2**............... singers

● Really need someone who can **3**...............

Time

● Meetings open at 6-8 p.m., every **4**...............

● Holiday time: **5**...............

Membership: includes a **6**............... every year

Membership fee

● Normal price: 40 pounds and 60 pence

● The unemployed and retired: **7**............... pounds

Maximum age for children: age of **8**............... and under

Regular types of plays

● Shakespeare

● **9**...............

● Christmas charity performance: The money raised will go to children's **10**...............

Part 2　*Questions 11-20*

Questions 11-14

Choose the correct letter, *A, B* or *C*.

Recycling Centre

Listening test audio

11. What should we do for the sake of the environment?

    A　not use metal paint

    B　not buy too much paint

    C　use up old paint

12. You can find out when your garbage will be collected at

    A　the customer service centre.

    B　instructions on the lid of the bin.

    C　the information desk.

13. How should you arrange the dustbins?

    A　leave some space between them

    B　leave them away from the cars in the parking lot

    C　leave them on the side of the road

14. How should you deal with bottles?

    A　smash them

    B　squash them flat

    C　take the tops off

Questions 15-20

Complete the table below.

*Write **ONE WORD** for each answer.*

Bin	Notes
yellow bin	for paper and **15**.............
white bin	put white goods (refrigerators, washing machines); **16**............. parts can be used
red bin	small domestic batteries and **17**............. batteries
brown bin	for glass (without any **18**.............)
purple bin	**19**............. cartridge (including **20**.............)

Test 1

3

Part 3   *Questions 21-30*

Questions 21-24

*Choose the correct letter, **A, B** or **C**.*

Listening test audio

21. Why does the man want to change the course?

    A   He wants to go abroad and work in other countries.

    B   He thinks the course is boring.

    C   The course is of no use.

22. What does the man think about the course Economics?

    A   It is similar to other courses.

    B   It is uninteresting.

    C   It is for more convenience in office work.

23. What's the woman's opinion about choosing Quantitative Analysis?

    A   It's too difficult for him.

    B   The man should choose it.

    C   It's optional.

24. Why does Anna want to learn a Foreign Language Course?

    A   to have fun while traveling

    B   to establish business relations with other countries

    C   She thinks it is useful for business and commerce.

Questions 25-26

*Choose TWO letters, **A-E**.*

What do they think about the lecturer?

    A   They think the professor (lecturer) should encourage students to have free thoughts.

    B   The professor is enthusiastic about the lectures.

    C   The professor doesn't teach much useful knowledge.

    D   The analytical method used by the professor is suitable for art students.

    E   The professor focuses on an in-depth study of one side of a problem.

Test 1

Questions 27-30

Matching four courses with their benefits.

*Choose your answers from the box and write the correct letter, **A-F**, next to Questions*
***27-30**.*

A	helps workers with cooperation
B	helps with speaking in public
C	helps reduce quarrels caused by the cultural differences
D	helps teamwork in large groups
E	helps with forming a clear plan for work
F	helps with predicting what others will say

27. Communication **1**   ....

28. Psychology   ....

29. Interpretation   ....

30. Communication **3**   ....

Part 4　　*Questions 31-40*

Questions 31-32

Choose the correct answer.

Listening test audio

Life in the world's oceans

31. Recent discoveries concerning marine life have been more accurate than earlier ones because scientists have

    A　studied a wide geographical area.

    B　included more information about the past.

    C　worked as a team on the project.

32. An international study has shed light on

    A　the effects of human activity on marine life.

    B　the extinction of a particular marine animal.

    C　the benefits of a marine conservation project.

Questions 33-38

Complete the flow-chart.

*Choose SIX answers from the box and write the correct letter, **A-I**, next to Questions 33-38.*

A	Alaska
B	fell
C	sea otters
D	kelp forest
E	flourished
F	fur trade
G	rose
H	sea urchins
I	villages

Fluctuating fortunes of the Alaskan kelp forests

2,500-4,000 years ago	otter numbers began to fall in areas around 33...............
	↓
	sea urchins reduced kelp in places
	↓
mid-1700s	start of 34..............
	↓
	otter numbers 35..............
	↓
	sea urchin numbers 36..............
	↓
	37.............. devastated
	↓
early 1900s	38.............. acquired protection
	↓
	sea urchin numbers declined
	↓
	kelp forests flourished

Questions 39-40

Complete the sentences.

*Write **NO MORE THAN TWO WORDS** for each answer.*

In recent times, **39**.............. have started feeding on sea otters.

In the near future, kelp forests are predicted to **40**..............

Test 2

Listening test audio

Part 1   *Questions 1-10*

Complete the notes below.

Write NO MORE THAN TWO WORDS AND/OR A NUMBER for each answer.

The Well-being Centre

Personal Information

- Name: Lily Swan
- Current job: **1**..............
- Contact number: **2**..............
- Height: 165cm
- Weight: 70kg

General Health

- frequent **3**..............
- occasional **4**..............
- allergic to: **5**..............
- now have problems with her **6**..............

Exercise Plan

Day	Activity	Duration	Location	Need to have
Monday	a brisk walk	**7**.............. minutes for the first few weeks	the **8**..............	training shoes and a hat
Tuesday	**9**..............	90 minutes	the **10**..............	comfortable clothes and a mat

Part 2   **Questions 11-20**

Complete the notes.

*Write **NO MORE THAN THREE WORDS AND/OR A NUMBER***

for each answer.

Listening test audio

The Heritage Trust (HT) Information Line

The public can visit 47 of the properties owned by the Heritage Trust.

Type of membership	Available to	Cost of membership (per year)	Special conditions
Individual	One adult	**£11**.............	
Senior	One person of **12**............. years or over	£21.20	Must send copy of **13**.............
Group	Groups larger than twelve	£190	Can't be used during **14**.............

Ways of joining:

● at any HT property office

● by post to

   -The HT Membership Department

   -PO Box 6547

   -**15**.............

   -Devonshire, **16**.............

Welcome pack includes

● **17**............. to all property sites

● opening times

● details about shows

Facilities now available for every property

● **18**............. (no payment for house visitors)

● shop

● **19**............. (specialising in local produce)

● tours of house (guided in four languages)

● own **20**............. for more details

Part 3   *Questions 21-30*

Questions 21-26

*Choose the correct letter, **A**, **B** or **C**.*

Listening test audio

21. What does Dr. Owens advise Joel to include in the title?

    A   the location of the specific farms he will investigate

    B   which country's agriculture he plans to research on

    C   what type of farming he's about to study

22. Why does Joel want to do a face-to-face interview?

    A   He can have a field investigation this way.

    B   He hopes to get a fuller answer.

    C   He wants to make friends with the farmers.

23. How will Joel investigate the influence of new technologies on farmers?

    A   by showing them a series of pictures

    B   by giving them a questionnaire

    C   by asking them open questions

24. Concerning government policies on farmers, the speakers agree that

    A   the government should increase its funding for agriculture.

    B   they are often irrelevant to farmers' actual needs.

    C   they don't support the development of new farming technologies.

25. According to Joel's reading, farmers

    A   don't know how to use new equipment.

    B   prefer to work alone.

    C   are not willing to try out new technologies.

26. A survey by Australian experts found that most of the farmers

    A   rely on a specialist to take care of their money.

    B   make changes based on limited research.

    C   are reluctant to cooperate with the government.

Test 2

Questions 27-30

What does Dr. Owens say about the following books?

*Choose **FOUR** answers from the box and write the correct letter, **A-F**, next to Questions 27-30.*

Description

A It's inaccurate.

B It's very boring.

C It fails to include a large number of samples.

D It's badly organised.

E It's out of date.

F It's too complicated.

Books

27. *An Overview of Agricultural Development in Human Society*

28. *How Do Government Policies Affect Farmers?*

29. *New Technologies in Modern Farming*

30. *How to Take Farming to the Next Level*

Part 4　*Questions 31-40*

Complete the notes below.

Write ONE WORD ONLY for each answer.

Listening test audio

The African Clawed Frog (Xenopus laevis)

Description

- Have **31** ....skin and vary in color
- Possess a layer of film for **32** ....
- Males are **33** .... the size of females

Habitat

- Native in Africa
- Live in water and prefer water that is **34** ....
- Can tolerate high levels of **35** .... in water
- Can't survive in water that contains metal
- In drought conditions: can live in **36** .... for a year

Diet

- Eat living or dead creatures in the water
- Use their sense of **37** ...., fingers, and a lateral line system to find food
- Use their front legs and a special **38** .... to move food into their mouths

More Information

- Many people in US keep them as a pet
- In some states, people consider them as a **39** ....
- Used in laboratories
- Useful for researches in early development
- Some mucus has **40** .... properties

Test 2

Test 3

Listening test audio

Part 1　　*Questions 1-10*

Complete the notes below.

Write ONE WORD AND/OR A NUMBER for each answer.

Children's Play Centre

Name: Children's Play Park

Age: from 6 months to **1**............. old

Fee: £1-£ 3.85

Do not need to **2**............. ahead of time

Facilities

- Separate sections with cushions for **3**............. to play on
- Several slides, **4**............. and tunnels
- A pitch where children can play basketball, **5**............. and volleyball

Classes

- Children are interested in dancing and **6**............. classes

Parties

- There will be a party host to organise performances and **7**.............
- For girls - a **8**............. party
- For boys - a pirate party (everyone can get a **9**............. and telescope)

Staff's phone number: 10.............

Test 3

Part 2　*Questions 11-20*

Choose the correct letter, A, B or C.

Listening test audio

Visiting Melville

11. Tips for taxi drivers and guides should be

   A　as generous as possible.

   B　as much as you feel is right.

   C　10% of the total fees.

12. What if you want medical help?

   A　You will be charged.

   B　Contact your personal insurance company.

   C　Find the hotel doctor.

13. What should you know about the water on the island?

   A　It contains no minerals.

   B　It's unsafe to drink.

   C　It has an unusual taste.

14. What does the woman say about the bottled water?

   A　It's sold everywhere.

   B　It often uses tap water.

   C　It's very expensive.

15. What are the buses like on the island?

   A　frequent

   B　punctual

   C　comfortable

16. How can you know for sure the buses' destination?

   A　You could check the number in front of the bus.

   B　You could find it at the bus stop.

   C　You could check with the driver.

17. How should you rent a car?

    A   compare the prices in advance yourself

    B   call a car-rental firm

    C   ask the hotel receptionist

18. What must you do when you collect the car?

    A   check the business license of the firm

    B   find out what is included in the price

    C   ask what special offers are available at the time

19. How can you find a taxi easily?

    A   book one online

    B   call the taxi rank

    C   stop one on the street

20. What should passengers know about the taxi fare?

    A   Taxi drivers run the meter and you pay the exact amount for it.

    B   Passengers should confirm the price with the driver before getting in.

    C   The price will be higher for night services.

Part 3   *Questions 21-30*

Questions 21-23

Choose **THREE** things the students decide to include in their seminar presentation.

Listening test audio

A	a short quiz
B	a short lecture
C	a slide presentation
D	some short readings
E	a small group talk
F	a small group discussion
G	some questions

Questions 24-30

Complete the notes.

Write **NO MORE THAN TWO WORDS** for each answer.

Seminar Outline

A. Establish problems

B. Concentrate on the **24**.............problems

C. Future situation

● production of **25**.............will decline

● tar sands and oil shale – no **26**.............problems, but produce pollution

D. Alternative energy sources

● **27**.............

● hydrogen

E. Objections

● too **28**.............

● difficult to generate power and to **29**............... it

● not suited to the design of present-day **30**.............

Test 3

Part 4   *Questions 31-40*

Questions 31-33

*Choose the correct letter, **A**, **B** or **C**.*

Listening test audio

31. The student chose to research Feininger's work because

   A   she had always admired his photographs.

   B   he took some well-known photographs of New York.

   C   he was famous as both architect and photographer.

32. How were Feininger's photographs different from those of other photographers?

   A   He showed the reality of life.

   B   He made cities look more beautiful.

   C   He photographed buildings from new angles.

33. Feininger left *Life* magazine because he wanted to

   A   take different kinds of photographs.

   B   publish his ideas and photographs.

   C   have more opportunities to travel.

Questions 34-36

Which exhibition took place in each of the following years?

Choose the correct answer for each year and move it into the gap.

Year	Exhibition
1955 **34**............ 1957 **35**............ 1977 **36**............	**A.** An exhibition focusing on his early work **B.** An exhibition devoted to his nature photographs **C.** An exhibition showing the development of his career **D.** An exhibition showing photographs taken for *Life* magazine **E.** An exhibition with other photographers

Questions 37-40

Complete the table.

Write **ONE WORD ONLY** *for each answer.*

Book title	Summary	Comment
New York in the Forties	Buildings in the city	Good examples of the 37 .... in photography
America Yesterday	City centres, suburbs and industrial areas Every photograph was taken 38	Information on how to use 39............. in photography
That's Photography	Most famous photographs	Contains two **40**........... about his work.

Test 3

Test 4

Listening test audio

Part 1   *Questions 1-10*

Complete the notes below.

Write ONE WORD AND/OR A NUMBER for each answer.

Holiday Activity Plan for Lily

	Activity	Location	Note
Mon.	Film		Cost: **1** £............. per ticket online Bring Lily some **2**.............
Tue.	A family **3**.............	The **4**.............	Arrive at **5**............. a.m. Bring Lily's **6**.............
Wed.	Party for Lily's **7**.............	A **8**............. (in High Street)	
Thur.	Music lesson	Huskey Hall	Don't forget to **9**.............
Fri.	Storytelling	A bookstore	Afterwards: Go to pick up laundry Buy some **10**.............

Part 2　*Questions 11-20*

Questions 11-15

*Choose the correct letter, **A**, **B** or **C**.*

Listening test audio

Auckland Environmental Project

11. Which type of environment is at the highest risk?

    A　beaches and seas

    B　mountains and hills

    C　rivers and lakes

12. What is special about Project Tiri?

    A　It's open to the public.

    B　Only native plants are grown in the area.

    C　It's the first forest planted by the volunteers.

13. What are volunteers for the project doing nowadays?

    A　scientific research

    B　planting trees

    C　guided tours

14. According to the speaker, what's the most important thing volunteers can gain from the project?

    A　educational benefit

    B　a sense of teamwork

    C　physical fitness

15. What should volunteers bring to the island?

    A　drink

    B　tools

    C　food

Test 4

Questions 16-20

What activity is recommended for each of the following conservation projects?

Choose FIVE answers from the box and write the correct letter, A-G, next to Questions 16-20.

Activities
A   Climb up the hills
B   Protect the birds
C   Pick up the litter
D   Work in water
E   Restore the buildings
F   Make paths
G   Plant vegetation

Projects

Great Mercury Island	16..............
Treasure Island	17..............
Coal Island	18..............
The Waikite Valley	19..............
Tuatapere Hump Ridge	20..............

Part 3　　*Questions 21-30*

Questions 21-25

*Choose the correct letter, **A**, **B** or **C**.*

Listening test audio

Study on the Bilingual Learning of Babies

21. What did Brian have trouble with while writing the paper?

  A finding enough information

  B structuring the content

  C focusing on one area

22. Why did Brian choose this topic?

  A People's attitudes towards bilingual learning have changed.

  B He has always been interested in the topic.

  C Not many other students have chosen this topic.

23. What negative belief did people originally have about bilingual education?

  A Bilingual children begin speaking later than their peers.

  B Bilingual children tend to mix up their two languages.

  C Bilingual children won't speak either of their languages as well as the native speakers of the languages.

24. What do both Brian and the tutor agree is the biggest advantage of bilingual learning for children?

  A They are more likely to have better employment opportunities in the future.

  B They tend to excel in school.

  C They are more capable of dealing with several tasks at the same time.

25. What is the biggest challenge for parents with bilingual children?

  A finding bilingual schools

  B planning bilingual hobbies

  C affording the fees for a bilingual education

Test 4

Questions 26-30

Write the correct letter, A, B or C, next to Questions 26-30.

A	had too few research participants
B	used new technology
C	surprising conclusion
D	poor data analysis
E	related to a global region
F	included lots of details

26. Richard Floridi   ....

27. Prof. Woodcock   ....

28. Prof. Granger   ....

29. Prof. Brito   ....

30. Maria Baralt   ....

Part 4　　*Questions 31-40*

Complete the table.

Write ONE WORD ONLY for each answer.

Listening test audio

Town Planning

Barningham now

- Population: 16,000

- Traditionally strong in the **31**............. industry

- Now the fastest developing industry is the **32**.............sector

- A major **33**.............company employs 600 people

- Transportation:

  -Road: busy near **34**.............

  -Train: infrequent

Future plan

- More new homes

- More new **35**.............

- A new scientific research park in collaboration with the local university

- Build a new **36**.............near the university

- Reduce **37**.............by 20%

- Encourage **38**.............in the city

- Floor space

  -10,000 sq metres for **39**............. use

  -8,000 sq metres for **40**.............use

Test 5

Part 1 *Questions 1-10*

Complete the notes below.

*Write **ONE WORD ONLY** for each answer.*

Listening test audio

Community Classes

Class / Day	Cost	Useful information	Need to bring
Guitar Thursday	$ 80	For beginners, the course starts at **1**............. a.m.	A guitar Something to **2**............. on
First Aid Tuesday	**3** $.............	Can sign up for another advanced course in the end and receive a qualification after passing all the tests	
Asian Cooking Wednesday	$ 60	Need to pay an extra **4** $............. for the ingredients Can get a manual and a **5**.............	Some containers A **6**.............
Tai-Chi Tuesday	$ 70		Loose clothes
Yoga Thursday	$ 70	Good for **7**.............problems	**8**.............
Make up Saturday	$ 38	Day and night makeup In **9**.............Community Centre	Makeup Brushes A small **10**.............

Part 2　　*Questions 11-20*

Questions 11-15

*Choose the correct letter, **A**, **B** or **C**.*

Listening test audio

Recreating the life in Iron Age

11. What did Jim say about a typical day in the village?

　　A　He feels cold at night.

　　B　He always gets up early.

　　C　He does not have enough time for himself.

12. What does Jim say about the breakfast there?

　　A　It takes time to prepare.

　　B　It is hard to get used to.

　　C　People finish eating quickly.

13. How is the evening meal in the village?

　　A　People are sometimes too tired to eat.

　　B　Their main food are fruits and berries.

　　C　People always talk about what they've done in the day.

14. What is the most important work of a blacksmith?

　　A　to mend tools and instruments

　　B　to maintain a stable source of heat

　　C　to collect food

15. What does Jim like the most about the village?

　　A　People have varied activities.

　　B　People share their knowledge.

　　C　People get a lot of exercise.

Test 5

Questions 16-20

Complete the flow chart below.

*Write the correct letter, **A-H**, next to Questions **16-20**.*

How to Build a Wooden Roundhouse

A	daub	**B**	different	**C**	equal	**D**	bones
E	scaffold	**F**	hazel	**G**	pegs	**H**	thatch

Mark the centre with the **16** ....

↓

Mark out a circle and the location of the posts

↓

Dig some holes using tools made of animal **17**............

↓

Drive the posts made of **18**............ into the holes

↓

Plant a stake in the centre

↓

Weave the fences with long, thin branches of hazel and oak trees

↓

Daub the walls with clay, sand, straw and manure

↓

Build up the roof with the help of the **19**............

↓

Tie up the rope around the roof poles and make sure they're of **20**............length

↓

Cover the roof with thatch

Part 3　　**Questions 21-30**

Questions 21-26

Choose the correct letter, A, B or C.

Listening test audio

21. What is the biggest shortcoming of the current definition of branding by AMA?

    A　It only focuses on sellers.

    B　It contains too much information.

    C　It's too narrow.

22. What do both students agree is the cause of the company's bankruptcy?

    A　The company changed its logo.

    B　The company did not adapt to the current situation.

    C　The company did not get enough funding support.

23. What does Sue want to learn about project management?

    A　how it works in a team

    B　its transferability to other aspects

    C　the constraints of the process

24. Why does Tom recommend the book to Sue?

    A　It's for those who already have some basic knowledge of this field.

    B　The content is precisely on re-branding.

    C　It's very clear.

25. What does Tom like about the passage Sue sent him by e-mail?

    A　It gives information about the historical use of focus groups.

    B　It offers practical information in forming a focus group.

    C　It can be used as a research model.

26. Why do those two students choose to focus on small companies?

    A　It's easier to conduct local research.

    B　They can find enough academic papers on small companies.

    C　They have first-hand experience in working in small companies.

Test 5

Questions 27-28

Choose TWO letters, A-E.

What are the **TWO** reasons for the failure of the re-branding of the ice cream company?

A   Its prices rose sharply.

B   It changed to a new ice cream formula.

C   It did not receive enough funding for a new logo.

D   It did not use enough colors in its new logo.

E   It adapted to a modern logo.

Questions 29-30

Choose TWO letters, A-E.

What are the **TWO** factors for the failure of the car-washing company?

A   It failed to monitor re-branding activities.

B   It changed its price structure.

C   It changed to an unpopular site.

D   It underestimated its competitors.

E   It refocused its marketing strategy to luxury.

Part 4　　*Questions 31-40*

Complete the notes.

*Write **ONE WORD ONLY** for each answer.*

Listening test audio

African Penguins

Location

- Live in the southern hemisphere on islands near southwest Africa

Adaptation to climate

- Need to keep the **31**............. of their bodies constant
- Restrict **32**............. on land to dawn and dusk
- Set up nests under tree **33**.............
- Spend most of the day swimming and use panting to keep cool

Other facts

- Unable to fly because of their heavy **34**.............
- Can dive to 130 metres deep and travel up to 110 km on land
- Annual moult: lose their **35**............. in almost three weeks

Threats to survival

- Rate of population drop - 80% in last 50 years
- Recent causes - industrial fishing and **36**.............
- Competition for **37**............. and for food with seals
- Natural predators - **38**.............

　　　　　　- sea lions

　　　　　　- seagulls (eat the penguins' **39**.............)

Recommendation for preservation

- Keep a strong **40**............. in genes

Test 6

Part 1 *Questions 1-10*

Complete the notes below.

Write ONE WORD AND/OR A NUMBER for each answer.

Test 6

Melbourne Sports Camp

General information

- There are baseball, tennis and **1**.............. classes
- They will be held in June
- The venue for the camp: at **2**.............. Street

Soccer class

- It aims to improve the children's skills and **3**..............
- Children do not need to bring any equipment (the staff will provide a **4**..............)
- Children should wear a **5**..............

Senior group activities

- A talk about **6**..............
- Entertainment activities: a talent show and a **7**.............. for them to enjoy
- The competition begins at **8**.............. on June 15th
- Name of the staff: Emma **9**..............
- Telephone number: **10**..............

Part 2   *Questions 11-20*

Questions 11-16

*Choose the correct letter, **A**, **B** or **C**.*

Listening test audio

Queensland Festival

11. Why does James recommend going there on Tuesday?

   A   Because the entrance is free.

   B   There are fewer people.

   C   It offers different educational classes.

12. The educational talk is held

   A   on weekends.

   B   every evening.

   C   every afternoon.

13. Why should people buy tickets in the library?

   A   It's cheaper.

   B   You'll receive a lovely book in advance.

   C   It's more convenient than buying a ticket in the city.

14. What may interest history lovers most is

   A   the garden.

   B   the architecture.

   C   the location.

15. What's special about the Cuisine Festival this year?

   A   It has a wider range of activities than before.

   B   A well-known musician will attend the festival.

   C   There will be luxury hotels and international chefs.

16. In the exhibition, visitors will be allowed to

   A   watch a display of how the steam engines work.

   B   dress up old uniform costumes.

   C   have a dinner inside the train cabinet.

Test 6

Questions 17-18

Choose TWO letters, A-E.

Which **TWO** are included in the family ticket?

    A   a toy

    B   a book for children

    C   a free meal on the train

    D   a guided tour to the Brisbane Tramway Museum

    E   a flag

Questions 19-20

Choose TWO letters, A-E.

Which **TWO** statements are true about the vote for the most popular event?

    A   People of any age can vote.

    B   People can vote through e-mail.

    C   Only local people can vote.

    D   People can vote several times.

    E   The voting will end at midnight on Saturday.

Part 4　　*Questions 31-40*

Question 31-36

Complete the notes.

Write ONE WORD ONLY *for each answer.*

Listening test audio

Project : Rural life in the early 13ᵗʰ century

Background

- period of great change: economy, society, technology
- research information obtained from:
- **31**.............. archives
- the Internet
- a **32**.............. found for him by librarians at the city library

Households

- 90% of population farming on small farms
- farms surrounded by a ditch (for **33**..............)
- richer people mainly bought pottery and spices (indicated by different types of **34**.............. in area)

Crops

- mainly cereals
- peas and beans **35**.............. the soil
- seeds had a casing of 'chaff' - guarded against disease and attacks by **36**..............

Questions 37-40

Choose the correct letter, A, B or C.

37. Crop mixing was an effective practice because it

    A made harvesting much quicker than before.

    B guaranteed yields despite weather problems.

    C kept the soil in an excellent condition.

38. The introduction of the heavy plough brought changes to

    A the type of seeds planted.

    B the type of animals used for ploughing.

    C the shape of the fields.

39. What was the innovation in windmills?

    A A new shape of sail was introduced.

    B People could move the sails to face the wind.

    C Sails could be removed more easily than before.

40. Small-holders got better crop yields than richer farmers because

    A only they knew about effective farming practices.

    B they planted crops which were well suited to the soil.

    C they had plenty of free labour easily available.

02

Section 2

雅思听力逐题
精讲解析

Test 1 解析

Part 1   *Questions 1-10*

场景介绍

主题场景	日常咨询	考查题型	笔记填空题
主旨大意	一位男士打电话咨询如何成为戏剧俱乐部会员		

逐题精讲

题型：**笔记填空题**

解析：此类题型一般由大标题、小标题、特殊印刷体（加粗或者斜体）以及并列信息构成，文章的层次结构非常清晰。考生可以快速浏览各级标题和各题题干中的关键词。因读题时间有限，考生切记不可过度翻译。有时笔记填空题的句子偏长、学术性词汇偏多，对此考生一定要提前画好空格前后的关键词，厘清句子主干，预读陌生单词，做好答案预测。在听录音的过程中，考生还要特别留意逻辑信号词，尤其是表示顺序、并列、总结、强调的连接词，这对于寻找答案很有帮助。

Question 1

题目定位词 / 关键词	117/155; Rehearsal address; House
录音原文定位	**MAN:** Well, first of all, I wonder where you usually rehearse. **WOMAN:** We've posted an address on our website. It's 117/155 Green Street, but that's our mailing address. *Actually, our rehearsals take place in the Club House.*
题目解释	根据题干可知，此处应填排练的地址。用数字 117/155 定位到接近答案的地方，紧接着下一句提到 rehearsal（排练），要找的答案是 House 前面的词，所以就是 Club。
答案	Club

Question 2

题目定位词 / 关键词	actors; singers
录音原文定位	WOMAN: Yes, we do. We've been recruiting members recently. You don't need to have any previous experience, but we're particularly in need of actors and male singers.
题目解释	根据题干可知，这里考查 and 连接的并列结构，考生要找与 actors 并列且修饰 singers 的词，所以答案应为名词或形容词。定位到答案句，和 actors 并列的词是 male singers, 所以答案就是 male（男性的）。
答案	male

Question 3

题目定位词 / 关键词	Really need someone; who can
录音原文定位	MAN: ...Do you have any special requirements? WOMAN: Yes, do you have a car? It's better if you can drive, because you know, for each play, there're always many stage props needed.
题目解释	根据题干可知，这里考查定语从句，Really need someone who can ...（真的需要某个能够……的人），考生要把重点放在 Really need 和 can 上，要找 can 后面的动词。根据小标题 Requirements 定位到男士提问是否有什么 special requirements，女士回答 it's better if you can drive，所以答案就是 drive（开车）。
答案	drive

Question 4

题目定位词 / 关键词	Meetings; 6-8 p.m.; every
录音原文定位	MAN: Haha. What about the hours? I'm afraid I won't be available on Thursdays because I have private tutoring lessons that day. I hope that's okay for you. WOMAN: Don't worry at all. Our routine meetings are on Tuesday every week. We start at 6 o'clock in the evening and end at 8 o'clock.
题目解释	根据题干可知，此处应该填写和时间有关的词。用 Meetings 可以定位到答案句，考生的目标是找会议时间。男士问时间，说自己周四可能没有时间，女士说在每周二开会，也就是 every Tuesday。
答案	Tuesday

Test 1 解析

Question 5

题目定位词 / 关键词	Holiday time
录音原文定位	MAN: Okay. I also wanna know, do we have to practice on holidays? Will there be any time off? WOMAN: Sure, there will. The club will be closed for 2 weeks in August, so you don't have to rehearse during that time.
题目解释	根据题干可知，此处应该填写假期的时间。这里用 holiday 定位，找俱乐部的假期，首先这位男士提到 Will there be any time off? 这里 time off 指的是休假，对应 holiday。下一句女士的回答中说 The club will be closed for 2 weeks in August，所以假期的时间是 August（8月），持续时间是 2 weeks。
答案	August/two weeks

Question 6

题目定位词 / 关键词	Membership; includes; every year
录音原文定位	MAN: Could you tell me more about the membership? What exactly does it include? WOMAN: Of course. Our members are pretty close to each other. We have a lot of group activities every year, including an annual dinner.
题目解释	根据题干可知，此处应该填写会员里包含的东西，且答案是单数名词。考生可以用 Membership 和 includes 定位。男士首先问你能告诉我更多关于会员 (membership) 的事吗？具体包括 (include) 什么？这里考生的目标是找"每年的一个……"，注意冠词 a，它意味着答案应该是单数名词。女士回答我们每年有很多群体活动，包括 an annual dinner。annual 表示"每年的"，同义替换 every year，所以答案是 dinner（晚餐）。
答案	dinner

Question 7

题目定位词 / 关键词	unemployed and retired; pounds
录音原文定位	MAN: That sounds interesting. I'd love to make some new friends. How much is your membership fee? WOMAN: Normally it's 40 pounds and 60 pence for each member, but if you currently don't have a job or have already retired, we will charge you only 25 pounds.
题目解释	根据题干可知，此处应该填写失业和退休的人需要交多少英镑的会员费，答案应为具体数字。男士提问 How much is your membership fee? 女士对不同类型的会员费用进行了回答。这里考生可以用并列结构 unemployed and retired 定位，unemployed（失业的）对应答案句中的 don't have a job，retired 原词重现，所以答案是 25/twenty-five 英镑。
答案	25/twenty-five

Question 8

题目定位词/关键词	Maximum age; children; age of; under
录音原文定位	**MAN:** That's a pretty fair price. It seems like your members cover a wide range of age groups. Are there any children in the association, too? My 15-year-old niece is also quite into theatre. Perhaps she could also become part of the Club? **WOMAN:** That's right. We pursue diversity in our association and welcome people of different ages from all walks of life to join us, but I'm afraid we have an age limit for children. We only accept minors aged 16 and younger.
题目解释	根据题干可知，此处应该填写关于孩子的年龄限制，需要填入一个具体的数字。男士说自己的侄女也想参加行不行，女士的回答里提到了年龄要求，答案句中的 age limit（年龄限制）对应 Maximum age（最大年龄）。这里提到的年龄是 16 and younger，也就是 16 岁及以下，所以答案是 16/sixteen。
答案	16/sixteen

Question 9

题目定位词/关键词	types of plays; Shakespeare
录音原文定位	**MAN:** That's all right. What kind of plays do you have then? **WOMAN:** Well, for the classics, we have Shakespeare, of course. Besides that, our members mainly focus on modern plays.
题目解释	根据题干可知，因为第 9 题在 Regular types of plays 这一标题下面，所以考生要找戏剧类型，并且答案要和 Shakespeare 并列。男士问你们有哪些戏剧类型，女士先回答有莎士比亚的，接着 Besides that（此外）提示并列对象出现，说他们的成员主要专注于现代剧，所以答案就是 modern plays。
答案	modern plays

Question 10

题目定位词/关键词	Christmas charity performance; money; children's
录音原文定位	**MAN:** That's great. Could you tell me more about your performances? **WOMAN:** No problem. Apart from the normal plays mentioned above, it's also our tradition to host a charity show every Christmas, from which all the money gathered will be donated to children's hospitals.
题目解释	根据题干可知，此处应该填写一个与小孩相关的名词，可能是某个地点或机构。用 Christmas charity performance 定位到答案句，考生是找募捐的钱将会去向孩子们的什么。答案句说收集到的钱将会捐给 children's hospitals，所以答案就是 hospitals（医院）。这里 gather（收集）同义替换 raise（筹集）。
答案	hospital(s)

Test 1 解析

场景词汇

单词	音标	词性	释义	单词	音标	词性	释义
address	/əˈdres/	n.	地址，住址	discount	/ˈdɪskaʊnt/	n.	折扣
rehearse	/rɪˈhɜːs/	v.	排练，排演	enquire	/ɪnˈkwaɪə(r)/	v.	询问，打听
require	/rɪˈkwaɪə(r)/	v.	需要，要求	rehearsal	/rɪˈhɜːsl/	n.	排练，预演
requirement	/rɪˈkwaɪəmənt/	n.	要求，必要条件	membership	/ˈmembəʃɪp/	n.	会员身份
actor	/ˈæktə(r)/	n.	演员	pound	/paʊnd/	n.	英镑
fee	/fiː/	n.	费用，会费	drama	/ˈdrɑːmə/	n.	戏剧，剧本
play	/pleɪ/	n.	戏剧	prop	/prɒp/	n.	道具
recruit	/rɪˈkruːt/	v.	招聘，招募				

拓展词汇

单词	音标	词性	释义	单词	音标	词性	释义
unemployed	/ˌʌnɪmˈplɔɪd/	adj.	未被雇用的，失业的	retire	/rɪˈtaɪə(r)/	v.	退休，退役
take place		phr.	发生	previous	/ˈpriːviəs/	adj.	以前的，先前的
vacancy	/ˈveɪkənsi/	n.	空缺，空职	driving license		phr.	驾照
available	/əˈveɪləbl/	adj.	可用的，有空的	private	/ˈpraɪvət/	adj.	私有的，私人的
tutor	/ˈtjuːtə(r)/	v.	辅导，教导；教学	time off		phr.	休假，请假
annual	/ˈænjuəl/	adj.	每年的，年度的	all walks of life		phr.	各行各业
limit	/ˈlɪmɪt/	n.	限制	gather	/ˈɡæðə(r)/	v.	聚集，收集
donate	/dəʊˈneɪt/	v.	捐赠，赠送				

Part 2　*Questions 11-20*

场景介绍 ▌

主题场景	活动介绍	考查题型	选择题（单项）+ 表格填空题
主旨大意	一位男士介绍为了环保大家应注意的事项以及垃圾箱分类		

逐题精讲 ▌

Questions 11-14

　　题型：选择题（单项）

　　解析：选择题（单项）解题的时候要把握好以下几个环节。

　　（1）在听录音前先找出题干和选项中的关键词，如名词、动词、副词、形容词等，在听录音的过程中，这些关键词能够起到定位的作用。

　　（2）审题时考生要抓紧时间辨别和理解选项的内容，把握选项的整体意思，尤其要关注选项中的形容词和动词，它们在录音中经常以同义替换的形式出现，如果选项比较长，最好画出关键词，方便进行细节比较。

　　（3）一般情况下，正确答案通常出现同义替换，尤其是涉及动词和形容词时；错误选项通常会原文重现，混淆视听，考生要多加辨析。

　　（4）表示转折的逻辑信号词（如but）、表示因果的逻辑信号词（如as）等出现的地方，很多时候都是答案设置点，考生务必额外关注。

　　（5）有时某个选项包含的动词或形容词会在录音中出现，要高度警惕该选项是否为干扰项。

Question 11

题目定位词 / 关键词	for the sake of the environment
录音原文定位	In order to be more environmental-friendly, I suggest you to buy just the amount of paint you need.
题目解释	题干：为了环境我们应该做什么？ A：不要使用金属油漆 B：不要买太多油漆 C：用完旧的油漆 用 for the sake of the environment 定位到答案句 in order to...environmental-friendly... 原文说为了更环保，建议你只买所需要的油漆量，正好对应选项 B。选项 A 只出现关键词 metal paint (Paints of all types, including metal paint, will be accepted and sent for re-use in the community)，其余表述与原文不一致。选项 C 未提及。
答案	B

Question 12

题目定位词 / 关键词	when your garbage will be collected
录音原文定位	The collection vehicles may travel different routes on some occasions, so the time your bin and recycling are collected may vary. The collection schedule can be found in the customer service centre.
题目解释	题干：你能在 _____ 知道你的垃圾什么时候会被收走。 A：客户服务中心 B：垃圾箱盖子上的说明 C：服务台 本题定位的重点在 when，考生要定位一个与时间相关的句子，答案句第一句 the time your bin and recycling are collected 提到了时间，接着第二句说"收集的时间表可以在客户服务中心找到"，正好对应选项 A。这里 time, schedule 都可以对应 when。选项 B 原文未提及相关信息。选项 C 与原文表述不一致，原文说的是如果找不到，可以问服务台（If you have problems finding it, you can ask the information desk for help... ）。
答案	A

Question 13

题目定位词 / 关键词	arrange the dustbins
录音原文定位	Also, please make sure that your bins are away from the roadside since traffic accidents may be caused by the waste bin falling down and rolling onto the road. In the normal course of things, trailers will come from the parking lot, so you should leave one metre's space, allowing trailers to pass between dustbins and collect garbage.
题目解释	题干：你应该如何安排垃圾箱？ A：在垃圾箱之间留出一些空间 B：让垃圾箱远离停车场的车子 C：把垃圾箱放在路边 当考生听到 make sure that your bins are away from the roadside（确保你的垃圾箱远离路边）时就应该意识到这里在讲垃圾箱的安排了，并且已经可以排除选项 C 了。答案句说"一般情况下，拖车会从停车场过来，所以你应该留出一米的空间，让拖车在垃圾箱之间通过，收集垃圾"，正好对应选项 A。选项 B 原文未提及。
答案	A

Question 14

题目定位词 / 关键词	deal with bottles
录音原文定位	Aside from the placement of dustbins, another thing you shouldn't forget is to remove the caps and lids on bottles and containers before recycling them.
题目解释	题干：你应该如何处理瓶子？ A：将它们砸碎 B：将它们压扁 C：把瓶盖摘下来 利用定位词找到答案句，答案句说"除了垃圾箱的放置位置，你不应该忘记的另一件事是在回收瓶子和容器之前取下盖子"，正好对应选项 C，这里 caps and lids 对应选项 C 中的 tops。选项 A 未提及。选项 B 与原文表述不一致，原文只提到 the water inside will affect the squashing process（里面的水会影响挤压过程），没有说需要把它们压扁。
答案	C

Questions 15-20

题型：表格填空题

解析：表格填空题旨在考查考生的听力基本功，通常需要考生填写国籍、地址、钱数、日期、时间及信用卡编号等。考生在听录音的时候要集中精神，注意细节和干扰性信息。建议考生平常多做基本功练习，避免在考试中因为基本功不扎实而丢分。

Question 15

题目定位词 / 关键词	yellow bin; paper and
录音原文定位	The yellow bin currently collects recyclable material from almost 96% of households. Paper and cards are accepted, such as newspapers, magazines, catalogues, contents of unwanted mail, telephone directories, yellow pages, cardboard and envelopes.
题目解释	根据题干可知，此处应填名词，且与 paper 并列。首先定位到 yellow bin 这个词，接着要找和 paper 并列的名词，对应到答案句 Paper and cards are accepted，这里和 paper 并列的名词是 cards，即为正确答案。
答案	cards

Question 16

题目定位词 / 关键词	white bin; white goods; parts
录音原文定位	On the right side of the yellow bin is a white bin, where you can dispose domestic white goods like refrigerators and washing machines. Even if they are old or damaged, some spare parts can still be put back into service after processing, so please keep them separated from scrap metal.
题目解释	根据题干可知，此处应填修饰 parts 的名词或形容词。首先定位到 white bin，原文说这里可以扔一些 white goods（大件家电）。考生的目标是找修饰 parts 的定语，紧接着下一句在说为什么要回收这些家电的时候就提到了 some spare parts，而且题干中的 can be used 也对应了原文的 put back into service（重新投入使用），题目要求只能填一个词，所以答案就是 spare（备用的，闲置的）。
答案	spare

Question 17

题目定位词 / 关键词	red bin; small domestic batteries and
录音原文定位	Opposite to the white bin, there is a red bin. It is for small household batteries and batteries from cars.
题目解释	根据题干可知，此处应填修饰 batteries 的名词或形容词。首先定位到 red bin，考生的目标是找和 small domestic batteries 并列的短语，并且空格后面的 batteries 需要被修饰。原文提到 It is for small household batteries and batteries from cars（这是用来收集小型家用电池和汽车电池的）。这里 small household batteries 就等同于 small domestic batteries（小型家用电池），and 后面能修饰 batteries 的词只有 car(s)。
答案	car(s)

Question 18

题目定位词 / 关键词	brown bin; glass; without any
录音原文定位	Remember to place the glass item in the correct coloured bin – the brown bin is for glass with no colour, the green bin is for brown glass, and green and blue glass should go into the blue bin.
题目解释	根据题干可知，此处应填一个名词。首先定位到说收集 glass（玻璃）的地方，这里说玻璃要放在正确颜色的垃圾箱里，接着后面具体说了什么颜色的玻璃放在什么颜色的垃圾箱。the brown bin is for glass with no colour（棕色的垃圾箱收集没有颜色的玻璃），这里 with no 对应题干中的 without any，所以答案就是 colour/color，两种拼写都可以。
答案	colour/color

Question 19

题目定位词 / 关键词	purple bin; cartridge
录音原文定位	And the last part is for cartridge recycling. Toner recycling is the latest raw material to make its way into the recycling chain and is important because the materials used to make ink and toner cartridges can be harmful to human health and the environment. Fortunately, nearly 100% of printer cartridge materials can be recycled. This greatly reduces airborne pollutants. You can drop your printer cartridge off at the purple bin and all types of toner cartridges will be accepted there, including ink.
题目解释	根据题干可知，此处需填入一个名词或形容词。本题定位范围比较广，最后一部分都在讲 cartridge recycling。考生要结合 purple bin 进一步定位，并且找修饰 cartridge（墨盒）的词，据此可定位到最后一句 You can drop your printer cartridge off at the purple bin（你可以将打印机墨盒丢进紫色垃圾箱），cartridge 前面的 printer（打印机）即为正确答案。
答案	printer

Question 20

题目定位词 / 关键词	including
录音原文定位	You can drop your printer cartridge off at the purple bin and all types of toner cartridges will be accepted there, including ink.
题目解释	根据题干可知，此处应填一个名词。第 20 题要跟第 19 题一起看，因为这里找的是第 19 题的 printer cartridge 的一个例子，定位词只有 including。本题和第 19 题定位到同一句话：You can drop your printer cartridge off at the purple bin and all types of toner cartridges will be accepted there, including ink（你可以将打印机墨盒丢进紫色垃圾箱，所有的墨粉盒都能丢在这里，包括墨水），所以答案是 including 后面的 ink（墨水）。
答案	ink

场景词汇

单词	音标	词性	释义	单词	音标	词性	释义
recycle	/ˌriːˈsaɪkl/	v.	回收利用，再利用	metal	/ˈmetl/	n.	金属
garbage	/ˈɡɑːbɪdʒ/	n.	垃圾	collect	/kəˈlekt/	v.	收集，采集
dustbin	/ˈdʌstbɪn/	n.	垃圾箱	smash	/smæʃ/	v.	打碎，粉碎
squash	/skwɒʃ/	v.	压扁，压碎	top	/tɒp/	n.	顶部，盖子

Test 1 解析

单词	音标	词性	释义	单词	音标	词性	释义
cap	/kæp/	n.	帽子，盖子	lid	/lɪd/	n.	盖子
battery	/ˈbætri/	n.	电池	waste	/weɪst/	n.	废弃物
environmental-friendly	/ɪnˌvaɪrənˈmentlˈfrendli/	adj.	对环境无害的，环保的	container	/kənˈteɪnə(r)/	n.	容器
category	/ˈkætəgəri/	n.	种类，范畴	dispose	/dɪˈspəʊz/	v.	处理，放置
packaging	/ˈpækɪdʒɪŋ/	n.	包装材料，外包装	pollutant	/pəˈluːtənt/	n.	污染物

拓展词汇

单词	音标	词性	释义	单词	音标	词性	释义
identify	/aɪˈdentɪfaɪ/	v.	认出，识别	material	/məˈtɪəriəl/	n.	材料，原料
domestic	/dəˈmestɪk/	adj.	家用的，家庭的	separate	/ˈseprət/	adj.	单独的，分开的
opposite to		phr.	与……相反	lithium	/ˈlɪθiəm/	n.	锂
flammable	/ˈflæməbl/	adj.	易燃的；可燃的	toxic	/ˈtɒksɪk/	adj.	有毒的
corrosive	/kəˈrəʊsɪv/	adj.	腐蚀的；侵蚀性的	reactive	/riˈæktɪv/	adj.	反应的
original	/əˈrɪdʒənl/	adj.	起初的，原先的	property	/ˈprɒpəti/	n.	性质，特质
cartridge	/ˈkɑːtrɪdʒ/	n.	（打印机的）墨盒	airborne	/ˈeəbɔːn/	adj.	在空中的，飞行中的
separate	/ˈsepəreɪt/	v.	区分，区别				

Part 3　*Questions 21-30*

场景介绍

主题场景	课程作业	考查题型	选择题（单项）+ 选择题（多项）+ 配对题
主旨大意	一个男士咨询选课的问题		

逐题精讲

Questions 21-24

　　题型：选择题（单项）

Question 21

题目定位词 / 关键词	Why; change the course
录音原文定位	SIMON: Well...I chose Literature at the beginning of this semester, but I'm considering whether to change it into Tourism Management in the next year. ANNA: Why? I think that Literature is pretty interesting. I still remember I looked forward to attending this class every time. SIMON: Yes, it sure is. But you know... I plan to study overseas in my senior year. And this course can help me work around the world, especially in New Zealand.
题目解释	题干：为什么这个男士想换课程？ A：他想去国外到其他国家工作 B：他觉得这个课程很无聊 C：这个课程没有用处 首先 Simon 提到这学期开始他选了文学课，但想改成旅游管理课。Anna 问他原因。Simon 回答说他计划出国学习，而且这个课程可以帮他在全世界工作，这正好对应选项 A，这里 study overseas 对应选项 A 中的 go abroad，work around the world 对应选项 A 中的 work in other countries。选项 B、C 在原文中均未提及。
答案	A

Test 1 解析

Question 22

题目定位词 / 关键词	man; Economics
录音原文定位	**ANNA:** I understand. Or maybe you can regard it as a plan B. Mm...let me see what else might be helpful to you. How about Finance or Economics? These sorts of courses can be useful wherever you go. **SIMON:** That's a good idea. But the problem is I have flipped through the course handout of Finance, and found it has many chapters that coincide with other courses I had. As for Economics...well, although it may allow me to have access to some office work, I still think it is boring and dull as a course, because I already learned it in high school and I have no interest in it.
题目解释	题干：这个人对经济学这门课程有什么想法？ A：它与其他课程类似 B：它很无趣 C：它是为了让办公室工作更方便 根据定位词首先定位到 Anna 问 How about Finance or Economics? Simon 接着回答他的感受，当听到 As for Economics 时才是他对 Economics 的感受，他说 I still think it is boring and dull（我还是觉得它很枯燥乏味）。这里 boring and dull 正好对应选项 B 中的 uninteresting，所以答案是选项 B。选项 A 描述的是 Finance，并不是 Economics。选项 C 原文未提及。
答案	B

Question 23

题目定位词 / 关键词	woman's opinion; Quantitative Analysis
录音原文定位	**SIMON:** Oh, I also saw that Quantitative Analysis was on the course list, but I heard that the final exam of the course is very difficult. Have you ever taken this class? **ANNA:** No, it's too challenging for me. The benefit is that you will get more credits than other courses. But, of course, that's under the premise of successfully passing the final exam. All in all, it's up to you, as it's an elective course.
题目解释	题干：女士对选择定量分析这门课程有什么想法？ A：这对他来说太难了 B：男士应该选择这门课 C：这是一门选修课 根据定位词 Quantitative Analysis 首先定位到 Simon 说的话，但是考生要找的是女士的观点，即 Anna 的观点才是重点。Anna 回答 All in all, it's up to you, as it's an elective course（总而言之，由你自己决定，因为这是一门选修课）。elective 正好对应选项 C 中的 optional（可选择的，选修的）。原文说这门课程对于 Anna 来说有挑战性（challenging），而不是对于男士来说有挑战性，故排除选项 A。选项 B 与原文不符，原文说的是让他自己决定。
答案	C

Question 24

题目定位词 / 关键词	Anna; Foreign Language Course
录音原文定位	**ANNA:** I'm going to take a Foreign Language Course. At first, I thought learning a foreign language would help enhance my travelling experiences. However, unfortunately, my travel plans have gone up the spout. **SIMON:** So why don't you change to another kind of course? **ANNA:** Actually I made this decision for another reason. I'm aiming at engaging in business after graduation since I find it useful. So I chose Chinese and Japanese, to be more specific, to facilitate business communication.
题目解释	题干：为什么 Anna 想学外语课程？ A：为了旅行时能玩得开心 B：为了与其他国家建立业务关系 C：她认为这对商业有帮助 根据定位词首先定位到 Anna 说她要学 Foreign Language Course 这门课的地方。紧接着她先说 At first, I thought ...（一开始，我觉得……），这里不是考生要找的答案，因为考生要找的是现在想学外语课程的原因。后面 Anna 提到了选这门课的另一个原因：I'm aiming at engaging in business after graduation since I find it useful.（我的目标是毕业后从事商业，因为我发现它很有用），正好对应选项 C。选项 A 是她之前选择外语课程的原因，但是现在情况有所改变。选项 B 原文未提及。
答案	C

Questions 25-26

题型：选择题（多项）

解析：解答这类题目时，考生一定要认真审题，确定正确答案的数量。多项选择题的出题规律一般是从5~6个备选项中选出2个正确答案或从7~8个备选项中选出3个正确答案。在听录音前，考生需要先找出题干和选项中的关键词，如名词、动词、形容词等，这些关键词能够起到定位作用，帮助考生迅速找到答案。多项选择题因选项较多，答题的难度也会增加，考生需要更加注意细节，注意选项信息之间的过渡及联系。除此之外，考生还要注意正确答案通常会发生同义替换，错误选项常会原文重现，要多加辨析。

题目定位词 / 关键词	they; lecturer
录音原文定位	**SIMON:** Right. That sounds helpful. Are the lectures given by Professor Smith? **ANNA:** Yes, he is also responsible for a course in the first year. **SIMON:** Oh, I'm having his course now and I really enjoy it. You can feel that he has a great passion for the class. **ANNA:** I agree. He always introduces all aspects of the research topic, so students will definitely gain a lot as long as they listen carefully. But that can also turn into a problem. His lecture is always teacher-centered. Students should be motivated to think critically. **SIMON:** Yeah, and as an art student, the analytical method adapted in his paper is too complex for me to apply.

题目解释	题干：他们对讲授者有什么看法？ A：他们认为教授（讲师）应当鼓励学生自由思考 B：教授对课程很热情 C：教授没有教什么有用的知识 D：教授使用的分析方法适合艺术学生 E：教授专注于对问题的一面进行深入研究 首先 Simon 问这些课都是 Professor Smith 讲吗，这里提到的 Professor Smith 对应题干中的 lecturer。确定他是授课老师后，Simon 道出了自己的想法，说 You can feel that he has a great passion for the class（你可以感受到他对课程有极大的热情），后面 Anna 也表示同意（I agree），所以这就是两人共同的观点。原文中的 passion（热情，激情）对应选项 B 中的 enthusiastic（热情的）。 接着 Anna 也陈述了自己的观点，But 转折引出 lecturer 的问题：His lecture is always teacher-centered（他的课都是以老师为中心的）；Students should be motivated to think critically（学生应该被鼓励进行批判性思考）。然后 Simon 回答说是的（Yeah），所以这也是两人共同的观点。这里对应选项 A，think critically 对应选项 A 中的 free thoughts。选项 C 原文未提及。选项 D 与原文不符，原文说的是 too complex for me to apply（太复杂了，应用不了）。选项 E 与原文描述不符，原文中 Anna 说的是 He always introduces all aspects of the research topic（他总是会介绍关于研究课题的所有方面）。
答案	A B

Questions 27-30

题型：配对题

解析：配对题要求考生对题干信息和选项信息进行匹配。这类题型的核心解题技巧主要包含三个方面。

（1）审题时考生一定要画出并记住每个选项的核心信息，在听录音的过程中，根据这些核心信息或其同义替换来选择正确答案（替换形式可以是单词之间的同义词、上下义、反义词的否定形式、同一单词的不同词性，也可以是句子转述）。

（2）熟悉题干中用于定位的词，最好在录音播放之前默念一遍题干。由于听力题目都是按顺序出题的，在听录音的时候，用题干信息来定位即可。

（3）用减负法或者笔记法辅助解题。减负法就是把听到的选项逐一画掉。在听录音的过程中加快浏览选项的速度，如果来不及浏览所有的选项，可以辅助标记一些笔记词，即录音中与题干关键词相关的内容。

对于配对题而言，看懂题目和听懂题目非常关键，如果听不太懂，敏感地识别出选项中的替换词也能够有效帮助考生定位和解题。一定要注意，配对题的选项极少会在录音中原词出现，考生在听到原文原词的时候应该多加辨析。最后，建议考生平时多积累和归纳替换词，提高考试时的反应速度。

Question 27

题目定位词 / 关键词	Communication 1
录音原文定位	**ANNA:** Wait a minute. I'm looking for the course list of our major. Here it is. Oh, I forgot Communication 1. **SIMON:** What's the course mainly about? **ANNA:** It helps you to overcome fear and deliver speeches smoothly, like how to organize the structure of your speech.
题目解释	用 Communication 1 首先定位到 Anna 说的话。紧接着 Simon 问这门课是关于什么的，Anna 回答说它可以帮助你克服恐惧，并且流利地进行演讲。这里 deliver speeches（演讲）对应选项 B 中的 speaking in public，所以答案为选项 B "帮助在公众场合讲话"。
答案	B

Question 28

题目定位词 / 关键词	Psychology
录音原文定位	**ANNA:** Yep, and there is Psychology. **SIMON:** I'm quite interested in it. Will this course teach us things about people's mental activities? **ANNA:** It will cover some of it. Well, the most practical part of it is Psychology promotes team cohesion, especially in a big group.
题目解释	Anna 提到了 Psychology，Simon 问这门课会教我们关于人们心理活动的事情吗？Anna 回答说这门课最实用的部分是会促进团队凝聚力，尤其是在大团队中。这里 team cohesion 对应选项 D 中的 teamwork，big group 对应 large groups，所以答案为选项 D "帮助大团队的团队协作"。
答案	D

Question 29

题目定位词 / 关键词	Interpretation
录音原文定位	**SIMON:** I see there is Interpretation. Is it similar to Communication 1? **ANNA:** Not really. It focuses on the conflicts in our daily life or work. For example, you can learn how to reduce the problems in collaborating with co-workers.
题目解释	Simon 提到了 Interpretation，问它和 Communication 1 相似吗？Anna 回答并非如此，它主要集中在日常生活和工作中的冲突上。听到这里可能会有考生选择选项 C "帮助减少由文化差异引起的争吵"，但是这里的冲突并没有提到是否由文化差异引起的，所以不能选 C。接着她又说这门课能够学习如何减少同事合作中出现的问题，正好对应选项 A "帮助同事之间合作"，collaborating 对应选项 A 中的 collaboration（合作）。
答案	A

Question 30

题目定位词 / 关键词	Communication 3
录音原文定位	**ANNA:** Then I'd recommend Communication 3. It guides us to notice the differences in cultures, which I believe could help us effectively deal with disputes brought by them.
题目解释	Anna 介绍 Communication 3，说它能指导我们注意到文化差异，这能帮助我们有效应对由此带来的争端，正好对应选项 C "帮助减少由文化差异引起的争吵"，这里 disputes（争端）对应选项 C 中的 quarrels（争吵）。
答案	C

场景词汇

单词	音标	词性	释义	单词	音标	词性	释义
course	/kɔːs/	n.	课程	economics	/ˌiːkəˈnɒmɪks/	n.	经济学
optional	/ˈɒpʃənl/	adj.	选修的	commerce	/ˈkɒmɜːs/	n.	贸易，商业
lecturer	/ˈlektʃərə(r)/	n.	演讲者，讲师	professor	/prəˈfesə(r)/	n.	教授
psychology	/saɪˈkɒlədʒi/	n.	心理学	semester	/sɪˈmestə(r)/	n.	学期
curriculum	/kəˈrɪkjələm/	n.	课程	literature	/ˈlɪtrətʃə(r)/	n.	文学
credit	/ˈkredɪt/	n.	学分				

拓展词汇

单词	音标	词性	释义	单词	音标	词性	释义
enthusiastic	/ɪnˌθjuːziˈæstɪk/	adj.	热情的	cooperation	/kəʊˌɒpəˈreɪʃn/	n.	合作
attend	/əˈtend/	v.	出席，参加	coincide with		phr.	符合；与……相一致
have access to		phr.	接近；可以利用	stalemate	/ˈsteɪlmeɪt/	n.	僵局；困境
enhance	/ɪnˈhɑːns/	v.	增强，提高	engage in		phr.	从事
passion	/ˈpæʃn/	n.	激情，热情	teacher-centered		phr.	以教师为中心
motivate	/ˈməʊtɪveɪt/	v.	激励，激发	deliver speech		phr.	发表演讲
cohesion	/kəʊˈhiːʒn/	n.	凝聚力，团结	persuasive	/pəˈsweɪsɪv/	adj.	有说服力的
collaborate	/kəˈlæbəreɪt/	v.	合作，协作	dispute	/dɪˈspjuːt/	n.	争端，争论
quarrel	/ˈkwɒrəl/	n.	争吵，争执	elective course		phr.	选修课

Part 4　　*Questions 31-40*

场景介绍 |

主题场景	自然环境	考查题型	选择题（单项）+ 流程图填空题 + 句子填空题
主旨大意	一场关于海洋生态系统的讲座		

逐题精讲 |

Questions 31-32

　　题型：选择题（单项）

Question 31

题目定位词 / 关键词	marine life; more accurate
录音原文定位	Now some of the predictions that were made initially turned out to be highly inaccurate, and it was suspected that this was due to insufficient historical data being available. So when a team of international scientists recently set out to reevaluate the state of various coastal ecosystems from Australia to Alaska, they were concerned to increase reliability by collecting as much of this kind of data as possible.
题目解释	题干：最近关于海洋生物的发现比以前的发现更准确，因为科学家们…… A：研究了广阔的地理区域 B：包括了更多关于过去的信息 C：作为一个团队参与了这个项目 根据关键词，考生可能会首先注意到这个句子：Now some of the predictions that were made initially turned out to be highly inaccurate, and it was suspected that this was due to insufficient historical data being available。这里提到一些最初做出的预测被证明是非常不准确的，有人怀疑这是由于历史数据不足。据此可以倒推出"现在更精确了，因为数据充足"，这对应选项 B。如果觉得不够严谨可以进一步往下听，they were concerned to increase reliability by collecting as much of this kind of data as possible。这个句子提到他们想通过收集尽可能多的数据来提高可靠性，这里 reliability 对应题干中的 accurate，data 对应选项 B 中的 information，所以可以确认答案为选项 B。
答案	B

Question 32

题目定位词 / 关键词	An international study; shed light on
录音原文定位	And when the extra dimension was included, the findings of the team were startling. Their studies demonstrated that there has always been a complex interaction between animals and plants living in our seas, between the top predators and the grazers and grassy plains of the ocean floors. We now know much more about what happens when humans intervene in this system. We know that playing with nature's ecosystems is extremely risky. You remove just one species of animal and it can have an impact on the whole system, often in an entirely unpredictable way.
题目解释	题干：一项国际研究揭示了…… A：人类活动对海洋生物的影响 B：某种海洋动物的灭绝 C：一个海洋保护项目的好处 考生要找的答案是国际研究的结果。当听到 the findings of the team were startling 时可预测接下来要讲具体的研究结果。第一个研究结果讲的是海洋动植物的互动，和选项无关。第二个研究结果是 We now know much more about what happens when humans intervene in this system，即我们现在知道当人类干扰这个（生态）系统的时候会发生什么，正好对应选项 A。
答案	A

Questions 33-38

题型：流程图填空题

解析：流程图填空题的答题方法与其他填空题基本一致。听录音前，考生需要对每道题目进行审题，思考单词的词性及与其余题目的逻辑关系。对于这种类型的题目，想要获得高分需要注意两点。

（1）注意录音中表示逻辑关系的词，因为题目和题目之间的连接是通过一定的逻辑关系来体现的。

（2）需要有一定的背景知识，因为流程图填空题通常出现在 Part 3 中，常考查论文写作、学术研究、毕业季找工作或者院校申请的过程，如果答题前对这些流程谙熟于心，则对于听力内容的把握会好很多。

Question 33

题目定位词 / 关键词	2,500-4,000 years ago; otter numbers began to fall; around
录音原文定位	And then somewhere between two and a half thousand to four thousand years ago when early people first occupied that region, the otter population began to decline. And it probably declined as a consequence of over hunting. However, the declines were relatively small in scale at that time and localized probably around village sites.
题目解释	通过 2,500-4,000 定位到出题点附近，根据题干可知，这里应填入一个地点，所以要特别注意听 around 或者它的同义替换词，如 about, roughly 等，在原文中 around 原词重现，其后面是 village sites，对应答案 I。
答案	I

Question 34

题目定位词 / 关键词	mid-1700s; start of
录音原文定位	In the mid-seventeen hundreds, the Alaskan Waters were discovered by the Bering Expedition and that set off the North Pacific fur trade.
题目解释	通过年份很容易定位到答案句，本题的重点是要找到 start 的对应词组 set off，意为"引起"，所以答案就是后面的 the North Pacific fur trade，对应选项 F。
答案	F

Question 35

题目定位词 / 关键词	otter numbers
录音原文定位	And as a consequence of that, otter populations were rapidly depleted to very low levels across the whole region.
题目解释	题目与 otter 的数量有关，答案大概率是上升了或者下降了，由此定位到答案句，答案句指出"结果，整个地区的 otter 数量迅速减少到非常低的水平"，对应选项 B，fell 和 depleted 都有"下降、减少"的意思。
答案	B

Question 36

题目定位词 / 关键词	sea urchin numbers
录音原文定位	And that in turn caused an explosion of sea urchin population and thus a collapse of the kelp forests.
题目解释	和上一题类似，这道题也问数量。定位到答案句，其中提到 an explosion of sea urchin population（海胆数量的暴增），explosion（爆炸，激增）对应选项 E flourished（兴旺，繁荣）。虽然选项 G rose 也有上升的意思，但相比较而言，flourished 能更好地体现 explosion 的意思。
答案	E

Question 37

题目定位词 / 关键词	devastated
录音原文定位	And that in turn caused an explosion of sea urchin population and thus a collapse of the kelp forests.
题目解释	这道题的定位词只有 devastate（毁坏，破坏），对应答案句中的 collapse（倒塌，崩塌），所以答案是 kelp forests，对应选项 D。
答案	D

Question 38

题目定位词 / 关键词	early 1900s; protection
录音原文定位	Then in the early nineteen hundreds before the Alaskan sea otters were completely wiped out, they became a protected species.
题目解释	考生的目标是找一个需要保护的东西。根据时间点定位到答案句，答案句说"20 世纪初，在 Alaskan sea otters 被完全消灭之前，它们成为了受保护物种"，也就是说 sea otters 需要保护，对应选项 C。
答案	C

Questions 39-40

题型：句子填空题

Question 39

题目定位词 / 关键词	feeding on sea otters
录音原文定位	In the late twentieth century, the unlucky sea otters began to decline again. Because this time they were being eaten by killer whales.
题目解释	根据题干可知，考生的目标是找一个以 sea otters 为食的物种。答案句说它们（sea otters）会被 killer whales 吃掉，所以答案就是 killer whales。
答案	killer whales

Question 40

题目定位词 / 关键词	kelp forests; are predicted to
录音原文定位	So as a result of this, the kelp forests can be expected to decline again since the sea urchin numbers are no longer controlled by the otters. And so the cycle continues.
题目解释	定位句说 kelp forests can be expected to decline，其中 be expected to 对应 are predicted to，所以答案就是 decline。
答案	decline

场景词汇 |

单词	音标	词性	释义	单词	音标	词性	释义
marine	/məˈriːn/	adj.	海洋的，海产的	extinction	/ɪkˈstɪŋkʃn/	n.	灭绝，消亡
sea otter		phr.	海獭	sea urchin		phr.	海胆
seaweed	/ˈsiːwiːd/	n.	海藻，海草	reduce	/rɪˈdjuːs/	v.	减少
devastate	/ˈdevəsteɪt/	v.	毁坏，破坏	feed on		phr.	以……为食
predict	/prɪˈdɪkt/	v.	预言，预计	ecology	/iˈkɒlədʒi/	n.	生态，生态学
coastal	/ˈkəʊstl/	adj.	海岸的	predator	/ˈpredətə(r)/	n.	捕食性动物；掠夺者
settlement	/ˈsetlmənt/	n.	定居点，聚居地	wipe out		phr.	消灭
killer whale		phr.	虎鲸				

拓展词汇 |

单词	音标	词性	释义	单词	音标	词性	释义
shed light on		phr.	阐明	formulae	/ˈfɔːmjʊliː/	n.	公式（复数形式）
equation	/ɪˈkweɪʒn/	n.	方程式	hurricane	/ˈhʌrɪkən/	n.	飓风
accurate	/ˈækjərət/	adj.	准确的，精确的	insufficient	/ˌɪnsəˈfɪʃnt/	adj.	不充分的，不足的
inaccurate	/ɪnˈækjərət/	adj.	不准确的，不精确的	fluctuate	/ˈflʌktʃueɪt/	v.	波动，起伏不定
intervene	/ˌɪntəˈviːn/	v.	干预，干涉	occupy	/ˈɒkjupaɪ/	v.	使用；占据
abundant	/əˈbʌndənt/	adj.	大量的，丰富的	graze	/greɪz/	v.	吃草；放牧
as a consequence of		phr.	由于……	deplete	/dɪˈpliːt/	v.	大量减少，耗尽
set off		phr.	引起	vibrant	/ˈvaɪbrənt/	adj.	充满活力的，充满生机的
collapse	/kəˈlæps/	n.	倒塌，塌陷	roller coaster ride		phr.	大起大落
tentative	/ˈtentətɪv/	adj.	暂定的				

Test 2 解析

Part 1 *Questions 1-10*

场景介绍

主题场景	运动健身	考查题型	笔记填空题 + 表格填空题
主旨大意	女士打电话给健康中心咨询如何减肥		

逐题精讲

Questions 1-6

题型：**笔记填空题**

Question 1

题目定位词 / 关键词	Current job
录音原文定位	**MAN:** Li-ly Swan. And, what's your current job? **WOMAN:** <u>Now I'm a nurse</u> and I am working in a hospital, but I plan to be a teacher one day, so I'm working on that. **MAN:** That's great. I'll just put "nurse" down here, and if you change your job in the future, we can update your information anytime.
题目解释	根据题干可知，本题应填女士目前从事的职业。录音中男士问女士目前的职业，关键词 current job 原词重现，根据女士的回答 I'm a nurse 即可得出答案。紧接着女士提到 teacher，但这是她计划去从事的职业，并不是目前从事的职业，后面再次提到 nurse 也可以帮助考生确定答案。
答案	nurse

Question 2

题目定位词 / 关键词	number
录音原文定位	**MAN:** And uh, could you tell me your phone number so we can get a hold of you? **WOMAN:** Yes, <u>my number is 0407 686 121.</u>
题目解释	根据题干可知，本题应填女士的电话号码。关键词 number 原词重现，答案随即出现。需要注意英文中数字 0 可以读作 zero 或者 o。
答案	0407 686 121

Question 3

题目定位词 / 关键词	General Health; frequent
录音原文定位	**MAN:** Okay. What about your general health? I have to know if you are currently suffering from any problems before I can design a training scheme for you. **WOMAN:** Well, I think overall I'm a healthy person. Oh, but I've been having these headaches quite often. Sometimes it really kills me.
题目解释	通过小标题 General Heath 可以预判后面要填女士的身体健康状况，并且是经常出现的状况。男士询问女士的身体状况如何？女士回答经常头疼，原文直接给出了答案，quite often 对应题干中的 frequent，答案为 headaches。
答案	headaches

Question 4

题目定位词 / 关键词	occasional
录音原文定位	**MAN:** I see. A lot of people also contract the flu easily during the flu season. Do you have the same problem? **WOMAN:** No, I'm alright. I seldom catch the flu, but I do suffer from colds from time to time.
题目解释	本题与上一题类似，可以预判这里要填女士偶尔会出现的一个身体状况。说完上一题的 headaches 之后，男士提到流感（flu），但女士说自己并没有这个问题，但是偶尔会 suffer from colds，由此得出正确答案为 colds。题干中的 occasional 对应原文中的 from time to time。
答案	colds

Question 5

题目定位词 / 关键词	allergic to
录音原文定位	**MAN:** Alright. Do you have any allergies then? **WOMAN:** Um, about that, I used to have an allergy to milk, but I've gradually outgrown it. Now I find myself allergic to seafood.
题目解释	根据题干可以预判这里应该填女士对什么物质过敏，需要填入一个名词。男士问女士有没有什么过敏的东西（allergies），女士的回答即为答案。女士提到之前对 milk 过敏，但是逐渐好了，现在对 seafood 过敏，题干中的 allergic to 原词重现。
答案	seafood

Question 6

题目定位词/关键词	now; problems
录音原文定位	MAN: Okay. Is that all I need to know about? Do you have any other things troubling you? WOMAN: Well, lately I also have sore eyes quite often. Perhaps it's because I work long hours and get too tired.
题目解释	根据题干可以预判这里应该填女士身体的哪一部分有问题，需填入一个名词。男士问是否还有什么事情困扰女士（things troubling you 与 have problems with 对应），女士的回答即为答案。女士说眼睛疼，所以答案为 eyes。
答案	eyes

Questions 7-10

题型：**表格填空题**

Question 7

题目定位词/关键词	brisk walk; Duration
录音原文定位	MAN: How long do you think you can keep going each time? WOMAN: I think, maybe 20 minutes. MAN: Why don't we set the bar higher? Let's say, 30 minutes at the beginning, and then after a few weeks, we can step it up to 45 minutes. WOMAN: Okay, I think I can manage that. We can have the walk in the school square.
题目解释	根据题干可以预判这里应该填健步走持续的时间，需填入一个数字。女士提到了 20 分钟，但是男士建议把时间延长到 30 分钟，女士表示赞同，即可得出答案。对话中表示后续可能延长到 45 分钟，但是这并不是刚开始几周的时长。
答案	30/thirty

Question 8

题目定位词/关键词	Location
录音原文定位	WOMAN: Okay, I think I can manage that. We can have the walk in the school square. MAN: Well, the school is fine, but isn't it a bit boring? Why don't we walk in a park? Is there any nearby? WOMAN: Yeah, I agree. Walking in a park is certainly much more interesting. There is a local park not far from my place.
题目解释	根据题干可以预判这里应该填在何处进行健步走，答案应为地点名词。女士首先提出 school，但是男士随后提出在学校走比较无聊，建议去 park，女士同意，即可得出答案。
答案	park

Question 9

题目定位词 / 关键词	Tuesday
录音原文定位	**MAN:** Good. Then on Tuesday, how about some yoga for 90 minutes? **WOMAN:** No problem. I like yoga. May I ask, where we are going to do this?
题目解释	根据题干可以预判这里应该填周二要做的运动，答案应为名词。Tuesday 原词重现，男士建议 yoga，女士表示没问题，即可得出答案。
答案	yoga

Question 10

题目定位词 / 关键词	Location
录音原文定位	**WOMAN:** No problem. I like yoga. May I ask, where we are going to do this? **MAN:** The sports centre is open. We can do yoga in there.
题目解释	根据题干可以预判这里应该填 yoga 的地点。第 9 题中女士表示同意后，马上问去哪儿做瑜伽，男士随后回答 sports centre，由此可得出答案。
答案	sports centre / sports center

场景词汇 |

单词	音标	词性	释义	单词	音标	词性	释义
well-being	/ˈwel biːɪŋ/	n.	幸福，安康	lose weight		phr.	减肥；体重减轻
general health		phr.	总体健康状况	suffer from		phr.	忍受，遭受
training scheme		phr.	培训方案	headache	/ˈhedeɪk/	n.	头痛
flu	/fluː/	n.	流行性感冒	cold	/kəʊld/	n.	感冒，伤风
allergic	/əˈlɜːdʒɪk/	adj.	对……过敏的	sore	/sɔː(r)/	adj.	（发炎）疼痛的，酸痛的
brisk walk		phr.	快步走	trainer	/ˈtreɪnə(r)/	n.	运动鞋
get hurt		phr.	受伤	yoga	/ˈjəʊɡə/	n.	瑜伽，瑜伽术

Test 2 解析

65

拓展词汇

单词	音标	词性	释义	单词	音标	词性	释义
current	/ˈkʌrənt/	adj.	现行的，当前的	from time to time		phr.	不时，有时
allergy	/ˈælədʒi/	n.	过敏反应，过敏症	outgrow	/ˌaʊtˈɡrəʊ/	v.	长大而不再具有
set the bar		phr.	定标准	step it up		phr.	更进一步
manage	/ˈmænɪdʒ/	v.	设法做到	square	/skweə(r)/	n.	广场
block	/blɒk/	v.	遮挡	mat	/mæt/	n.	地垫，垫子
loose	/luːs/	adj.	（衣服）宽松的				

Part 2　*Questions 11-20*

场景介绍 |

主题场景	商业经营		考查题型	笔记填空题
主旨大意	对遗产信托机构的介绍			

逐题精讲 |

　　题型：**笔记填空题**

Question 11

题目定位词 / 关键词	Cost; individual
录音原文定位	We offer several different types of membership. The individual membership is our most popular with an annual cost of twenty nine pounds fifty.
题目解释	根据题干可以预判这里应该填写个人会员每年的费用，答案应为数字。当从录音中听到 We offer several different types of membership 时即预示着接下来将开始介绍不同的会员类型。首先提到了 individual membership，individual 和 cost 在定位句中原词重现，annual 同义替换 per year，答案随即出现。
答案	29.50/29.5

Question 12

题目定位词 / 关键词	Senior; years
录音原文定位	But we also have a senior plan and that's available for individuals who are 58 years and above...
题目解释	根据题干可以预判这里应该填写对 senior 会员的年龄要求，答案应为数字。原文介绍完 individual membership 后马上提到了 senior plan，senior 和 years 原词重现，above 同义替换 over，所以年长会员办卡的年龄要求在 58 岁及以上。
答案	58/fifty eight

Question 13

题目定位词 / 关键词	copy
录音原文定位	Obviously we would not require you to produce proof of age every time you visit a property, but we do ask that when you register for a senior membership, you send us a photocopy of your passport.
题目解释	根据题干可以预判这里应该填写 senior 会员需要某个东西的复印件，答案应为名词。原文中 photocopy 同义替换 copy，答案随即出现。
答案	passport

Question 14

题目定位词 / 关键词	Can't be used during
录音原文定位	The total cost is 190 pounds and can be used at any time throughout the week including weekends. But unfortunately we are unable to allow visits on National Holidays under this plan.
题目解释	根据题干可以预判这里应该填写团体会员在什么期间无法使用，应该填入某个时间。录音中说完 group 会员的费用为 190 英镑之后，先说可以在一周当中任意一天使用，然后用 But 进行转折，说出无法在 National Holidays 的时候使用。
答案	National Holidays

Question 15

题目定位词 / 关键词	PO Box 6547
录音原文定位	We offer two different ways to apply for membership... And you can also join by post. Please write to the HT Membership Department. PO Box six five four seven. And that's in Beanham. Spelled B-E-A-N-H-A-M, which is in Devonshire, PL twenty three nine PU.
题目解释	根据小标题可知，这里要填入第二种加入会员的方式，即邮寄时需要填写的相关信息，可以预判这里应该填寄送地点。当从录音中听到 We offer two different ways to apply for membership 时预示着将要开始介绍申请方式。当听到 And you can also join by post 时预示着答案即将出现，根据录音对字母进行听写即可。
答案	Beanham

Test 2 解析

Question 16

题目定位词 / 关键词	Devonshire
录音原文定位	And you can also join by post. Please write to the HT Membership Department. PO Box six five four seven. And that's in Beanham. Spelled B-E-A-N-H-A-M, which is in Devonshire, PL twenty three nine PU.
题目解释	同上题，这里依旧问邮寄的地点。当录音中出现 Devonshire 后，根据录音对字母和数字组合进行听写即可，但要注意题目的字数要求。
答案	PL239PU

Question 17

题目定位词 / 关键词	Welcome pack; all property sites
录音原文定位	Upon joining us you will receive a welcome pack which has a wealth of useful information about the trust and its properties. It includes directions to all HD properties.
题目解释	根据小标题可以预判这里应该填 welcome pack 包含的内容。welcome pack 一词出现后，提到的第一个包含的内容为 directions（指南），all HD properties 对应 all property sites，即可确定答案。
答案	directions

Question 18

题目定位词 / 关键词	no payment
录音原文定位	We are now able to guarantee that all heritage trust properties offer the following facilities to visitors: car parking, which is free to all visiting the house—just keep your entrance ticket or membership card and show it on exit...
题目解释	根据小标题可以预判这里应该填写向访客免费开放的设施。录音中 facilities 一词出现后，car parking 是第一个提到的设施，随后听到的 free 同义替换题干中的 no payment，all visiting the house 同义替换题干中的 house visitors，由此可确定答案。
答案	car parking

Question 19

题目定位词 / 关键词	shop; local produce
录音原文定位	...a special heritage trust shop selling a wide range of top quality merchandise; <u>a restaurant with particular emphasis on locally produced food and guided tours in four European languages.</u>
题目解释	根据题干可以预判这里应该填写出现在 shop 之后的向游客开放的设施，答案应为名词。录音中 shop 原词重现后，紧接着出现的第一个名词为 restaurant，随后出现的 locally produced 对应 local produce，即可确定答案。
答案	restaurant

Question 20

题目定位词 / 关键词	own
录音原文定位	...and guided tours in four European languages. For up-to-date information, <u>each house now has its own website.</u> Just do a search under the name of the house.
题目解释	根据题干可以预判这里应该填写出现在 tours of house 这一信息点之后提供的一项设施，答案应为名词。录音中 own 原词重现，more details 对应 up-to-date information，答案即为 website。
答案	website

场景词汇

单词	音标	词性	释义	单词	音标	词性	释义
preserve	/prɪˈzɜːv/	v.	保护，维护	property	/ˈprɒpəti/	n.	所有物，财产，房产
national importance		phr.	国家重要性	membership	/ˈmembəʃɪp/	n.	会员身份
register	/ˈredʒɪstə(r)/	v.	登记，注册	photocopy	/ˈfəʊtəʊkɒpi/	n.	复印件；影印本
form	/fɔːm/	n.	表，表格	welcome pack		phr.	欢迎礼包
direction	/dəˈrekʃən/	n.	方向，方位	facility	/fəˈsɪləti/	n.	设施，设备
merchandise	/ˈmɜːtʃəndaɪs/	n.	商品，货品	staff	/stɑːf/	n.	全体员工

拓展词汇 |

单词	音标	词性	释义	单词	音标	词性	释义
heritage	/ˈherɪtɪdʒ/	*n.*	遗产	charge	[tʃɑːdʒ]	*v.*	要价，收费
enclose	/ɪnˈkləʊz/	*v.*	附上	senior	/ˈsiːniə(r)/	*adj.*	年长的
guarantee	/ˌɡærənˈtiː/	*v.*	确保，保证	proof	/pruːf/	*n.*	证明
committed to (doing)		*phr.*	致力于做……				

Part 3　*Questions 21-30*

场景介绍

主题场景	课程作业	考查题型	选择题（单项）+ 配对题
主旨大意	一位学生向导师询问关于政府政策和新科技对农业的影响的研究论文的意见		

逐题精讲

Questions 21-26

题型：**选择题（单项）**

Question 21

题目定位词 / 关键词	advise; include in the title
录音原文定位	**Joel:** Yes, I will mainly focus on Australia. Right, maybe I should point that out in the title. **Dr. Owens:** Hmm, perhaps it'd be better if you could carry out a case study of a certain area and then narrow it down to several particular farms. Specify the place in your title so it won't seem too general. **Joel:** That's a great idea. I can investigate the different types of farming in an eastern town and interview the farmers.
题目解释	题干：Dr. Owens 建议 Joel 在标题中加入什么内容？ A：他要研究的农场的位置 B：他想要研究哪个国家的农业 C：他想要研究的农业类型 Joel 提到要在 title 中指出要研究 Australia 的情况，接着导师给出了自己的建议。导师建议缩小到研究几个农场，并且在题目中详细说明这些农场的地点。particular farms 同义替换选项 A 中的 specific farms，the place 同义替换 location，specify 与题干中的 include 意思相同，故选项 A 正确。选项 B 是由学生自己提出的，并非导师的建议。选项 C 同样由学生提出，并且未提及要加入标题中。
答案	A

Question 22

题目定位词 / 关键词	face-to-face
录音原文定位	**Dr. Owens:** Certainly. How do you plan to interview them? On the phone or face-to-face? **Joel:** I prefer the latter method. **Dr. Owens:** Why is that? Is that because you want to see the farms yourself? **Joel:** A face-to-face interview does allow me to do that, but that's not really my intention. From my experience, people don't like to discuss serious things on the phone, so they usually cut their answers short and sometimes even don't say what they really mean. By talking directly to the farmers, I'm more likely to get a complete response from them.
题目解释	题干：Joel 为什么想做面对面的访谈？ A：这样他可以进行田野调查 B：他希望得到一个更全面的回答 C：他想跟农民们做朋友 根据题干中的 face-to-face 可定位到相关内容。学生表示与农民们直接交谈更容易得到更完整的回答，complete response 同义替换选项 B 中的 fuller answer，故选项 B 正确。选项 A 由导师提出，但是后续学生否定说并不是他的意图。选项 C 是 face-to-face interview 可能带来的结果，并非原因，故排除。
答案	B

Question 23

题目定位词 / 关键词	influence; new technologies
录音原文定位	**Dr. Owens:** And you mentioned new technologies. When you're in the field, how exactly will you find out their influences on the farmers? **Joel:** I guess I'll just show them some pictures of modern farming, and then ask them how they feel about them. **Dr. Owens:** Well, pictures can be vivid and direct, but I'd say it's better to avoid being so specific. Similarly, instead of giving them a questionnaire with leading questions, you can just start with some general questions. This can help you avoid influencing them and allow them to answer the question in their own way that reveals their true thoughts. **Joel:** You're right. I'll change my method then.
题目解释	题干：Joel 是怎么调查新科技对农民的影响的？ A：通过向他们展示一系列的图片 B：通过给他们一个调查问卷 C：通过询问他们一些开放性的问题 本题可以通过 new technologies 来定位。录音中导师问学生打算用什么方法调查新科技对农民的影响。学生说要展示图片，然后问他们的感受。但是导师紧接着建议他最好不要这么具体（排除选项 A），而且比起给他们 questionnaire，不如用 general questions 来提问，排除选项 B。选项 C 中的 open questions 对应 general questions，学生接受了导师的意见，故选择选项 C。
答案	C

Test 2 解析

Question 24

题目定位词 / 关键词	government policies
录音原文定位	**Dr. Owens:** You also mentioned the government's role in agriculture. What information have you gathered so far? **Joel:** Yes, I've done some research online trying to find out what policies have been made in this area. From what I've learnt, the government is actually quite supportive of the agricultural industry, though the results are not very satisfying. The investment in farming has been on the rise these years and they also encourage the farmers to introduce new farming equipment and technologies. **Dr. Owens:** Right, these are all measures that try to increase the total grain output, but despite their good intentions, they forget to address the real problems and desires of farmers in face of the new changes. **Joel:** I couldn't agree more...
题目解释	题干：关于政府对农民的政策，说话的人赞同以下哪个观点？ A：政府应当增加对农业的资助 B：它们常常与农民的实际需求无关 C：它们无法为新的农业技术提供支持 导师问关于政府的角色学生收集到了什么信息。学生提到了政府的一些政策，包括增加对农业的投资，鼓励农民引进新的农业设备和科技，导师回应说虽然这些政策意图是好的，但是政府的政策忽视了农民们的实际问题和诉求，对应选项 B 中的 irrelevant to farmers' actual needs，随后学生也表示了赞同，故选择选项 B。学生提到这些年对于农业的投资一直在增加，并且鼓励农民去使用新设备，这些表述与选项 A、C 矛盾，故排除。
答案	B

Question 25

题目定位词 / 关键词	Joel's reading
录音原文定位	**Joel:** I couldn't agree more. Based on what I've read, many of them actually wish to try out some new farming equipment and technologies, but end up flinching back because of how complicated they appear. And since they don't really understand their value, they consider it a mere waste of money. They would rather work with the whole family or employ some workers instead to increase the output.
题目解释	题干：根据 Joel 所阅读的资料，农民有什么表现？ A：不知道如何使用新设备 B：更愿意自己干 C：不愿意尝试新技术 通过录音中的 what I've read 定位，学生提到大多数人是想尝试新设备和新技术的（排除选项 C），但最终因为它们太难操作而退缩了，对应选项 A。他们宁愿举家之力或雇用别人来代替机器，故排除选项 B。
答案	A

Question 26

题目定位词 / 关键词	Australian experts
录音原文定位	**Dr. Owens:** That's a shame, isn't it? More guidance should be given to the farmers on how to keep pace with the new era. I remember reading a research paper by a group of Australian experts. According to them, the vast majority of farmers are, in fact, willing to work with the government and adapt to the modern way. However, most of them don't know how to gather information and usually rush into making some wrong adjustments that produce bad results.
题目解释	题干：澳大利亚专家的调查发现大多数的农民怎么样？ A：依靠专家来管理他们的钱 B：根据有限的研究做出改变 C：不愿意与政府合作 通过 Australian experts 可定位到谈论调查的句子，导师指出农民们大多不知道怎样搜集信息就匆忙做出错误的决定，making some wrong adjustments 同义替换选项 B 中的 make changes，故选项 B 为正确答案。原文中并未提到靠专家来管钱，故排除选项 A。原文中说农民们愿意和政府合作（willing to work with the government），与选项 C 的描述相矛盾，故排除选项 C。
答案	B

Questions 27-30

题型：配对题

Question 27

题目定位词 / 关键词	*An Overview of Agricultural Development in Human Society*
录音原文定位	**Dr. Owens:** Sure. Not every book is worth reading. Let me see... Well, firstly, I wouldn't recommend *An Overview of Agricultural Development in Human Society*. Though many say it's a must-read if you want to learn about the history of agriculture, it's really dull and many students won't make it to the second chapter.
题目解释	本题通过书名定位。dull 同义替换 boring，对应选项 B。
答案	B

Question 28

题目定位词 / 关键词	*How Do Government Policies Affect Farmers*
录音原文定位	**Dr. Owens:** And, you can remove this one from your list—*How Do Government Policies Affect Farmers*. It has several interesting ideas regarding the influences of the government, but the whole book is a mess. The author tries to appear smart by using a lot of big words and jargons, but in fact the content of each section is loosely put together and the logic between them just doesn't hold.
题目解释	本题通过书名定位。is a mess，loosely put together，doesn't hold 都表示整本书很混乱，没有逻辑，对应选项 D"条理不清"。
答案	D

Question 29

题目定位词 / 关键词	New Technologies in Modern Farming
录音原文定位	**Dr. Owens:** Well, New Technologies in Modern Farming, this one definitely has to go. **Joel:** Why is that? **Dr. Owens:** I've read the book before, and to my surprise, there were many mistakes in the content, like the chapter introducing farm automation.
题目解释	本题通过书名定位。导师提到这本书里有很多 mistakes，对应选项 A 中的 inaccurate。
答案	A

Question 30

题目定位词 / 关键词	How to Take Farming to the Next Level
录音原文定位	**Dr. Owens:** That's right. Oh, and this one, How to Take Farming to the Next Level. You can skip it. It used to be one of the required readings and even the textbook for those majoring in agriculture, but that was two decades ago. The examples it uses are too old and some analyses don't apply to the current situation.
题目解释	本题通过书名定位。导师提到书里用的例子太旧，而且不适合现在的情况，too old 和 don't apply to the current situation 都对应选项 E 中的 out of date。
答案	E

Test 2 解析

场景词汇

单词	音标	词性	释义	单词	音标	词性	释义
agriculture	/ˈæɡrɪkʌltʃə(r)/	n.	农业	title	/ˈtaɪtl/	n.	名称，标题
carry out		phr.	执行，实行	case study		phr.	案例研究
narrow	/ˈnærəʊ/	v.	（使）变窄；压缩	specify	/ˈspesɪfaɪ/	v.	明确指出，具体说明
general	/ˈdʒenrəl/	adj.	综合的，广泛的	investigate	/ɪnˈvestɪɡeɪt/	v.	调查，研究
intention	/ɪnˈtenʃn/	n.	意图，目的	field	/fiːld/	n.	现场，实地
questionnaire	/ˌkwestʃəˈneə(r)/	n.	问卷，调查表				

拓展词汇

单词	音标	词性	释义	单词	音标	词性	释义
complete	/kəmˈpliːt/	adj.	完全的，完整的	vivid	/ˈvɪvɪd/	adj.	生动的，逼真的
reveal	/rɪˈviːl/	v.	揭示，透露	grain	/greɪn/	n.	谷物，谷粒
output	/ˈaʊtpʊt/	n.	产量	flinch back		phr.	退缩
adapt to		phr.	使适应于	rush into		phr.	仓促行动
adjustment	/əˈdʒʌstmənt/	n.	调整	undermine	/ˌʌndəˈmaɪn/	v.	逐渐削弱（损害）
jargon	/ˈdʒɑːgən/	n.	行话，黑话	loosely	/ˈluːsli/	adv.	松散地

Part 4 *Questions 31-40*

场景介绍

主题场景	动物植物	考查题型	笔记填空题
主旨大意	对非洲爪蛙的介绍		

逐题精讲

题型：**笔记填空题**

Question 31

题目定位词 / 关键词	skin
录音原文定位	African clawed frogs <u>have very smooth skin,</u> which can change its color to adapt to the environment.
题目解释	根据题干可以预判这里应该填修饰皮肤的形容词。录音中与皮肤相关的形容词为 smooth，后面也提到了颜色会改变，对应题干中的 vary in color，由此可确定答案。
答案	smooth

Question 32

题目定位词 / 关键词	layer
录音原文定位	Their skin is covered with thick mucus <u>which forms a layer of film. It can prevent excess water from entering the body and thus serves as a way of protection.</u>
题目解释	根据题干可以预判这里应该填这层薄膜的作用，答案应为名词。录音中 layer of film 原词重现，serves as a way of protection 表示起到一种保护作用。
答案	protection

Question 33

题目定位词 / 关键词	Males; size
录音原文定位	Male frogs are much smaller than the female ones. An adult female frog is about 4 inches long, whereas <u>a male frog only measures 2 inches, which means it's half as long as the female one.</u>
题目解释	根据题干可以预判这里应填雄性爪蛙与雌性爪蛙的体型比较。male 和 female 原词重现，录音中提到雄性爪蛙只有 2 英寸长，是雌性爪蛙的一半长，也就是大小只有雌性爪蛙的一半。原文中的 long 对应题干中的 size。
答案	half

Question 34

题目定位词 / 关键词	water
录音原文定位	Nevertheless, they prefer to live in still water, which means they don't like running streams and you're more likely to see them in the stagnant ponds or lakes.
题目解释	根据题干可以预判这里应该填爪蛙喜欢居住的水环境的特征，答案应为形容词。录音中根据 water 定位，可知爪蛙更喜欢在静水（still water）中生活，后面的 stagnant（不流动的）也表达了相同的意思，由此可得出答案。
答案	still / stagnant

Question 35

题目定位词 / 关键词	tolerate; water
录音原文定位	African clawed frogs are very tolerant to changes in the environment and will survive in almost any body of water. For example, they can live in water that contains a high level of salt.
题目解释	根据题干可知这里应填水中含有的某种物质，答案应为名词。high level of 原词重现，答案即为 salt。
答案	salt

Question 36

题目定位词 / 关键词	drought
录音原文定位	Though they usually live in the water, during droughts, they can also burrow into the mud, becoming dormant for up to a year.
题目解释	根据题干可知这里应该填爪蛙可以生存一年的某种环境或地点，答案应为名词。drought 一词可以用来定位，其在原文中原词重现，burrow into 同义替换 live in，即可确定答案为 mud。for a year 对应原文中的 for up to a year，据此可再次确认答案。
答案	mud

Question 37

题目定位词 / 关键词	sense; fingers
录音原文定位	They rely on their acute sense of smell and extremely sensitive fingers to locate and catch their prey. They also have a lateral line system on both sides of the body, which gives them the ability to sense movements and vibrations in the water and help detect the prey.
题目解释	根据题干可知这里应该填爪蛙用来找寻食物的某种感官，答案应为名词。在听到小标题下第一行的关键词 living, dead, water 等词后，可知录音中即将出现与爪蛙饮食相关的内容。随后 sense of 原词重现，答案随即出现，原文中的 rely on 对应题干中的 use。随后听到的 fingers, lateral line 也可再次确认答案。
答案	smell

Question 38

题目定位词 / 关键词	front legs, special
录音原文定位	In the feeding process, since African clawed frogs do not have tongues, they use their forelimbs and a special pump to press food into their mouths for consumption.
题目解释	根据题干可知这里应填爪蛙特有的某个把食物送进嘴里的部位,答案应为名词。而且,要填入的词与 front legs 构成并列关系,所以可以通过 front legs 定位。front legs 对应原文中的 forelimbs，and a special 原词重现，答案即为 pump。
答案	pump

Question 39

题目定位词 / 关键词	consider...as
录音原文定位	However, though they're popular in the US, in some states like California, African clawed frogs multiply rapidly and act like an invasive species that negatively affects other species in the freshwater ecosystems. That's why they are treated as a type of pest in these places.
题目解释	根据题干可知这里应填在某些国家人们把爪蛙视为什么，答案应为单数名词。在听到本题所在的小标题下的关键词 US, pet 后，可知录音中马上要提到与本题相关的内容。录音中提到在某些洲爪蛙像入侵物种，对淡水生态系统有负面影响，所以人们把它视为害虫，treated as 同义替换 consider...as，答案随即出现。
答案	pest

Question 40

题目定位词 / 关键词	mucus; properties
录音原文定位	One of the most significant protections of African clawed frogs against their ever-changing environment are the compounds secreted by their skin, such as some mucus with antibiotic properties.
题目解释	根据题干可知这里应填它们的黏液有什么性质，答案应为形容词或名词。根据 mucus 定位，properties 原词重现，答案随即出现。
答案	antibiotic

场景词汇

单词	音标	词性	释义	单词	音标	词性	释义
clawed	/klɔ:d/	adj.	有爪或螯的	amphibian	/æmˈfɪbiən/	n.	两栖动物
renowned	/rɪˈnaʊnd/	adj.	有名望的，著名的	streak	/stri:k/	n.	条纹
mucus	/ˈmju:kəs/	n.	黏液	layer	/ˈleɪə(r)/	n.	薄层
indigenous	/ɪnˈdɪdʒənəs/	adj.	本土的	aquatic	/əˈkwætɪk/	adj.	水生的，水栖的
still	/stɪl/	adj.	静止的	burrow	/ˈbʌrəʊ/	v.	掘地洞，钻到……下面
forelimb	/ˈfɔ:lɪm/	n.	前肢	pump	/pʌmp/	n.	泵

拓展词汇

单词	音标	词性	释义	单词	音标	词性	释义
monochrome	/ˈmɒnəkrəʊm/	adj.	单色的	stagnant	/ˈstæɡnənt/	adj.	不流动的
discharge	/dɪsˈtʃɑ:dʒ/	v.	（使）排出；（使）流出	container	/kənˈteɪnə(r)/	n.	容器
scavenger	/ˈskævɪndʒə(r)/	n.	食腐动物	invasive	/ɪnˈveɪsɪv/	adj.	侵入的
neural plate		phr.	神经板	embryo	/ˈembriəʊ/	n.	胚，胚胎
antibiotic	/ˌæntibaɪˈɒtɪk/	adj.	（与）抗生素（有关）的	wound	/wu:nd/	n.	创伤，伤口

Test 3 解析

Part 1 *Questions 1-10*

场景介绍

主题场景	活动咨询		考查题型	笔记填空题
主旨大意	一位女士打电话咨询儿童游乐场的设施、兴趣课及活动等相关信息			

逐题精讲

题型：**笔记填空题**

Question 1

题目定位词 / 关键词	6 months
录音原文定位	**WOMAN:** That's nice. But my children are young, only about three years old. I don't know if it is suitable for them to play here. **MAN:** That shouldn't be a problem. <u>Our equipment is designed for children aged 6 months to 11 years.</u>
题目解释	根据题干可知，此处需要填写年龄。题干问的是对年龄的限制，从 6 个月到多少岁，6 months 是一个关键的定位词。由于数字是比较容易抓取的信息，据此可以很快在录音中定位到年龄，答案即为 11 years。
答案	11 years

Question 2

题目定位词 / 关键词	not; ahead of time
录音原文定位	**WOMAN:** Uh huh. Do I need to make reservations two or three days in advance? I'm afraid that there will be no room left. **MAN:** It covers a large area. <u>Most of the time the space is enough, so you don't have to book in advance.</u>
题目解释	根据题干可知，此处需要填写一个动词。题干的意思是不需要提前做什么。女士问需不需要 make reservations（预订），怕教室不够，男士回答不需要，空间足够。注意题干中的否定词 not 及 ahead of time。在听力原文中，也出现了表示否定的 don't，而 in advance 同义替换题干中的 ahead of time，所以根据上下文的意思，这里需要填写的动词是 book，即不需要提前预订。
答案	book

Question 3

题目定位词 / 关键词	Facilities; Separate sections...for
录音原文定位	**WOMAN:** OK, that sounds good. Are there any facilities for kids to explore new activities? **MAN:** Sure. We have many different entertainment areas and some are only open to babies. These areas are filled with cushions, so they can have fun on them. And cushions are also used to protect them from getting injured. You can rest assured that children's safety will be of paramount importance.
题目解释	根据题干可知，这道题属于 Facilities 的类别，此处需要填写一个名词。当听到 facilities 时预示着马上要开始介绍儿童乐园的设施了。题干的意思是"有单独的配有垫子的区域提供给……玩耍"，对应听力原文的"我们有许多不同的娱乐区，有些只对婴儿开放"，所以这里需要填写的名词是 babies。后文提到的 These areas are filled with cushions 也再次确认了该答案。
答案	babies

Question 4

题目定位词 / 关键词	slides; tunnels
录音原文定位	**MAN:** We have built many entertainment devices to improve children's fitness, such as slides, which are one of children's favorite things to play with. Also, there are some bridges and tunnels, which train their sense of balance.
题目解释	根据题干可知，空格处的单词与其前后的名词 slides 及 tunnels 构成并列结构，都是儿童乐园的设施，而且都被 several 修饰，所以空格处所填写的单词大概率也是一个复数名词。原文提到 slides 后，马上介绍了 bridges and tunnels，即可确定这里需要填写的名词是 bridges。
答案	bridges

Question 5

题目定位词 / 关键词	pitch; basketball; volleyball
录音原文定位	**MAN:** We certainly do. Actually, it's a pitch where they can play all kinds of ball games, including basketball. If there are more than five kids, we will also help to organize football and volleyball matches.
题目解释	根据题干可知，空格处的单词与其前后的名词 basketball 及 volleyball 构成并列结构，所以空格处所填写的单词大概率也是一个表示体育运动的名词。根据关键词 pitch 进行定位，basketball 和 volleyball 原词重现，则另一项体育运动即为 football。
答案	football

Test 3 解析

Question 6

题目定位词 / 关键词	dancing; classes
录音原文定位	WOMAN: Oh, do you have any classes? MAN: Yes. What kind of classes are you looking for? WOMAN: My daughter has indulged in singing these days. I wonder if it's possible for her to join a music class? MAN: I'm so sorry. We haven't had any music classes yet. But we do have dancing classes. And another course, drama, is also well-liked by almost all kids. You can ask your daughter if she is interested in it.
题目解释	根据题干可知，这道题属于 Classes 的类别，空格处需要填写的内容是某个课程，逻辑上与 dancing 并列。当听到女士询问有没有课程时即可预判接下来要展开介绍儿童乐园具体有哪些课程了。女士先问有没有音乐课程，男士回答没有，然后提到了他们有的两个课程，分别是 dancing classes 和 drama，所以需要填写的单词是 drama。
答案	drama

Question 7

题目定位词 / 关键词	Parties; host to organise performances
录音原文定位	WOMAN: Alright. How about parties? Will there be any parties? MAN: Absolutely. We have different theme parties every week. In these parties, children are encouraged to perform in public to show their talents. The party host will also arrange some games for the children to improve their sense of cooperation.
题目解释	根据题干可知，这道题属于 Parties 的类别，此处需要填写一个与 performances 并列的名词。女士询问有没有 parties 后，男士回答有，在 parties 上孩子们可以在公众面前表演，perform 对应题干中的 performances，下一句的 also 引出 parties 的另一个活动，即 arrange some games，organise 同义替换 arrange，and 等同于 also，所以空格处需要填写的单词是 games。
答案	games

Question 8

题目定位词 / 关键词	girls; party
录音原文定位	MAN: Because they have distinct interests and hobbies, we will organize parties for girls and boys separately. For girls, they can pose with fun props like a lion tamer's flaming hoop. WOMAN: Flaming hoop...That sounds like a circus party, isn't it?
题目解释	根据题干可知，空格处填写的是修饰 party 且与 girls 有关的名词或形容词。涉及到听力原文的两句话，第一句话提到 girls，预示答案即将出现，第二句话则与答案有关，party 前面的 circus 即为答案。
答案	circus

Question 9

题目定位词 / 关键词	boys; a pirate party; telescope
录音原文定位	WOMAN: What about boys? MAN: Boys will enjoy a pirate party. Before the party, everyone will receive a telescope and a hat, so that they can play the part of pirates and immerse themselves in the party.
题目解释	根据题干可知，空格前的冠词 a 预示着空格处大概率应填一个单数名词，且与 telescope 并列。根据 boys 和 pirate party 即可定位答案句，get 同义替换原文中的 receive，telescope 原词重现，与其并列的 hat 即为正确答案。
答案	hat

Question 10

题目定位词 / 关键词	phone number
录音原文定位	MAN: I will help you sign up for membership. Could you tell me your phone number? Oh, and we will assign you a private customer service staff. If you have any problems, don't hesitate to contact him. His telephone number is 016 1962 3388.
题目解释	根据题干可知，空格处需要填写电话号码。注意听力原文出现电话号码的地方即可，并且要注意说话人是否会修改说出的数字。
答案	016 1962 3388

场景词汇 |

单词	音标	词性	释义	单词	音标	词性	释义
advertisement	/əd'vɜːtɪsmənt/	n.	广告	arrange	/ə'reɪndʒ/	v.	安排
equipment	/ɪ'kwɪpmənt/	n.	设备；器材	circus	/'sɜːkəs/	n.	马戏团，马戏表演
price	/praɪs/	n.	价格	serve	/sɜːv/	v.	提供
reservation	/ˌrezə'veɪʃn/	n.	预留，预订	membership	/'membəʃɪp/	n.	会员身份
book	/bʊk/	v.	预订	sign up		phr.	注册
facility	/fə'sɪlɪti/	n.	设施				

拓展词汇

单词	音标	词性	释义	单词	音标	词性	释义
in advance		*phr.*	提前	prop	/prɒp/	*n.*	道具
cushion	/ˈkʊʃən/	*n.*	垫子	tamer	/ˈteɪmə/	*n.*	驯服者
paramount	/ˈpærəmaʊnt/	*adj.*	首要的；至上的	pirate	/ˈpaɪərɪt/	*n.*	海盗
slide	/slaɪd/	*n.*	滑梯	telescope	/ˈtɛlɪskəʊp/	*n.*	望远镜
indulge	/ɪnˈdʌldʒ/	*v.*	沉迷	immerse	/ɪˈmɜːs/	*v.*	沉浸在，深陷于
well-liked	/wel laɪkt/	*adj.*	很受欢迎的	assign	/əˈsaɪn/	*v.*	分配，指定
sense of cooperation		*phr.*	合作意识				

Part 2　　*Questions 11-20*

场景介绍 |

主题场景	旅游度假	考查题型	选择题（单项）
主旨大意	一位女士回答听众咨询有关 Melville 这个岛屿的旅游信息，包括出行、医疗、饮水及小费等		

逐题精讲 |

题型：选择题（单项）

Question 11

题目定位词 / 关键词	Tips for taxi drivers and guides; generous; you feel; 10%
录音原文定位	But for taxi drivers or guides, you're free to tip any amount you want.
题目解释	题干：应该怎么给出租车司机和导游小费？ A：尽可能大方 B：随意给 C：全部费用的 10% 根据题干可知，这道题与给司机和导游小费有关，原文从 The first letter is from Jenny. She's curious about giving tips for taxi drivers and guides 开始介绍给司机和导游小费的问题。随后的听力原文中提到 you're free to tip any amount you want，也就是说你可以随意给，所以答案为选项 B，原文中的 free to tip any amount you want 在答案中被替换成了 as much as you feel is right。值得注意的是，原文在提及给司机和导游小费前说在当地的餐厅和理发厅需要给小费，小费通常是消费总额的 10%（when you're in a restaurant or hair salon here, usually the tip is about 10%），这部分内容容易让人误会，误选选项 C。所以，看清题目的定位 / 关键词是做对听力题目的重要一步。此外，要注意说话人是否使用了表示转折的词或词组，如这里的 But，有转折就表示会有变化，需要进一步确认。选项 A 是导游们希望乘客这么做的（the guides may expect you to give a lot），但实际上乘客并不需要这么做。
答案	B

Test 3 解析

Question 12

题目定位词 / 关键词	medical help; charged; personal insurance company; hotel doctor
录音原文定位	Jenny is also asking about what one should do if she needs a doctor. <u>Well, firstly, you need to know that there will be a charge.</u>
题目解释	题干：如果需要医疗救助会怎么样？ A：你需要付费 B：打给你的保险公司 C：找酒店的医生 这道题问的是需要医疗救助时会怎么样。听力原文从 Jenny is also asking about what one should do if she needs a doctor 开始介绍与医疗有关的内容。第一，医疗要花钱（there will be a charge）；第二，有说英语的医生，但需要自己支付医疗费（pay the medical bills yourself）；第三，最好提前买好保险，等生病受伤了就来不及了（buy some medical insurance before coming here; too late to call the insurance company after you get hurt or sick）；第四，不要找酒店里的医生（don't call the hotel doctor）。根据这些内容，只有选项 A 是符合要求的，be charged 同义替换 there will be a charge。选项 B 和 C 的内容在听力原文中被否认了。
答案	A

Question 13

题目定位词 / 关键词	water on the island; no minerals; unsafe; unusual taste
录音原文定位	Firstly, of course the tap water is safe to drink, so you don't have to worry at all. It's just that there are some minerals in it, <u>so it may taste a bit strange to some people,</u> like our Alice. It's not harmful. You'll get used to it, or you can choose to buy bottled water instead.
题目解释	题干：关于岛上的水，你应该知道什么？ A：不包含矿物质 B：饮用不安全 C：有一股奇怪的味道 根据题干可知，这道题与岛上的水有关，听力原文从 She mentions one thing particular—the drinking water on the island 开始介绍相关内容。首先提到岛上的自来水是安全的 (the tap water is safe to drink)；其次提到水里有矿物质，所以喝起来会有点怪（there are some minerals in it, so it may taste a bit strange to some people）；最后说这个水是无害的（It's not harmful），不喜欢的人可以买瓶装水（buy bottled water instead）。根据这些内容，只有选项 C 符合要求，unusual taste 替换 taste a bit strange。选项 A 和 B 与听力原文内容相悖，所以排除。
答案	C

Question 14

题目定位词 / 关键词	bottled water; everywhere; uses tap water; expensive
录音原文定位	Alice says you can find it in almost every corner of the island and the price is not high, so it's really convenient. But she also reminds us that sometimes people might simply put the tap water into a bottle for sale.
题目解释	题干：关于瓶装水女士说了什么？ A：到处都有卖的 B：经常用的是自来水 C：非常贵 根据题干可知，这道题与瓶装水有关，听力原文从 or you can choose to buy bottled water instead 开始介绍瓶装水。随后提到瓶装水到处都可以找到且价格不贵（find it in almost every corner of the island and the price is not high）。但有时候会有猫腻，会有人用自来水冒充瓶装水（put the tap water into a bottle），所以需要注意。根据这些内容，只有选项 A 符合要求，sold everywhere 与 find it in almost every corner of the island 意思相同。选项 B 和 C 的内容与原文不符，所以排除。
答案	A

Question 15

题目定位词 / 关键词	buses; like; Frequent; Punctual; Comfortable
录音原文定位	She also talks about the buses. Well, there are not many buses on the island but they are all very reliable, because they stick to a fixed schedule and always arrive on time. But you should be prepared for the bumpy roads here. The journey might not be as smooth as you imagine.
题目解释	题干：岛上的巴士是怎么样的？ A：很频繁 B：很准时 C：很舒适 根据题干可知，这道题与巴士有关，需要选择一个符合当地巴士特征的形容词。听力原文中说那里的巴士不是很多（not many），但可靠（very reliable），因为有固定的时间表（stick to a fixed schedule），到达也准时（arrive on time）。此外，原文中还提到道路颠簸（bumpy roads）及路程不舒服（might not be as smooth as you imagine）。根据这些内容，只有选项 B 符合要求，punctual 同义替换 stick to a fixed schedule and always arrive on time。选项 A 和 C 的内容与原文不符，所以排除。尤其注意选项 C，巴士舒适与否出现在 But 之后，转折后的内容会和之前的内容形成对比。
答案	B

Question 16

题目定位词 / 关键词	sure the buses' destination; check the number; at the bus stop; check with the driver
录音原文定位	So, if you want to know where a bus is heading and where it will stop along the way, it's best that you go and ask the driver directly.
题目解释	题干：你怎样确定巴士的终点站？ A：你可以检查巴士前面的数字 B：你可以在巴士站看到 C：你可以跟司机确认 根据题干可知，这道题与确认巴士的目的地有关。一开始听力原文提到巴士会在前面显示目的地，但会错（Sometimes it might just show the destination instead, but that can also be wrong），注意转折词 but。此外，巴士还会跳站（the bus might not pull over at some stops）。随后补充说最好的方法是直接询问司机（it's best that you go and ask the driver directly）。根据这些内容，选项中只有 C 符合要求，check with 替换 ask。选项 A 和 B 都有可能出错，所以排除。
答案	C

Question 17

题目定位词 / 关键词	how; rent a car; Compare the prices; car-rental firm; hotel receptionist
录音原文定位	Find out the prices of different companies and then choose the best option among them.
题目解释	题干：你如何租车？ A：提前比较价格 B：打给租车公司 C：问酒店的接待员 这道题询问如何租车，听力原文从 He wants to find some information about the car renting services here 开始介绍租车的问题。后续提到不能仅仅依靠租车公司 (don't just call a rental company and hope that they will take care of everything)，因为这些租车公司会联系不上 (can't get through to them) 且收费过高 (overcharge you)。此外，酒店的接待员也不可信 (Don't turn to the hotel receptionist either)。随后提出正确的做法（Here's what you should do），即找到不同公司的价格，然后从中选择最佳的（Find out the prices of different companies and then choose the best option among them）。根据这些内容，本题只有选项 A 正确。选项 B 和 C 均不建议，所以排除。
答案	A

Question 18

题目定位词 / 关键词	must you do; collect the car; business license; what is included in the price; special offers
录音原文定位	But when you go to fetch the car, make sure they clarify with you about all the content of the services you've bought with them.
题目解释	题干：当你取车时要做什么？ A：检查租车公司的营业执照 B：确认价钱包含的内容 C：询问当前的优惠活动 这道题问的是取车时的注意事项。听力原文从 when you go to fetch the car 开始介绍相关内容。前面说了这些公司都是合法的（lawful businesses）、有资质的（have all the certificates required for operation），不用担心售后（don't have to worry about the after-sale service）。然后用 but 进行转折，提到了需要注意的事情：clarify with you about all the content of the services you've bought with them，即明确你所购买的服务的所有内容，这些内容包括无限里程（unlimited mileage）、免费地图（free maps）、季节性促销活动（seasonal promotions）等。根据这些内容，只有选项 B 符合要求，find out 替换 clarify。
答案	B

Question 19

题目定位词 / 关键词	find a taxi easily; Book one online; Call the taxi rank; Stop one on the street
录音原文定位	Just go and flag down the one passing by you. It's the quickest way.
题目解释	题干：你如何容易地找到一辆出租车？ A：在网上预订 B：打电话给出租车站 C：在街上拦一辆 这道题与打出租车有关，听力原文从 But instead of renting a car, he prefers getting a taxi 开始讲述打出租车的内容。首先说的是出租车很多，很容易叫到（availability won't be a problem because there are enough taxis in most places），接着说因为车多所以不需要网上预订或者提前预订（you don't have to reserve it online or call a taxi rank），最后说最快的方式就是走到路上拦一辆（Just go and flag down the one passing by you. It's the quickest way）。纵观这些内容，只有选项 C 符合要求，stop one 替换原文中的 go and flag down the one，easily 替换原文中的 quickest。
答案	C

Test 3 解析

Question 20

题目定位词 / 关键词	passengers know about the taxi fare; run the meter; confirm the price; higher for night services
录音原文定位	Considering that, my advice is, you should ask the driver how much the ride is gonna cost and reach an agreement with him right at the beginning.
题目解释	题干：关于出租车的费用乘客应该知道什么？ A：出租车司机打开计价器，乘客根据计价器的准确价格付费 B：乘客应该在上车前与司机确认价格 C：夜间服务的价格会更高 随着上一题的结束，听力原文开始说车费的问题（As for how much they will charge you...），并提到很多人希望能够根据路程来计价 (many people would agree that the fairest way is to charge according to distance, so they'd turn on the meter after you get in the car)，但注意这里出现了转折词 but，要特别关注转折词后的内容。原文说实际上这里有一些车没有计价器（some taxis here don't have a meter），所以排除选项 A，有些人甚至需要在到达目的地时支付额外的费用，特别是在晚上（pay extra money when they arrive at the destination, especially at night），也就是说无论白天还是夜晚都可能会价格过高（排除选项 C），所以建议一开始就和司机商定好价格（you should ask the driver how much the ride is gonna cost and reach an agreement with him right at the beginning），选项 B 符合原文内容，reach an agreement 对应题干中的 confirm，at the beginning 对应题干中的 before getting in。
答案	B

场景词汇

单词	音标	词性	释义	单词	音标	词性	释义
tip	/tɪp/	n./v.	小费（一般以 tips 复数形式出现）/ 给小费	fetch the car		phr.	取车
charge	/tʃɑːdʒ/	n./v.	收费，要价	clarify	/ˈklærɪfaɪ/	v.	澄清
tap water		phr.	自来水	availability	/əˌveɪləˈbɪlɪti/	n.	可用性，有用性
car renting		phr.	租车	reserve	/rɪˈzɜːv/	v.	预订
overcharge	/ˌəʊvəˈtʃɑːdʒ/	v.	过高要价	meter	/ˈmiːtə/	n.	计价器
certificate	/səˈtɪfɪkɪt/	n.	证书，合格证				

拓展词汇

单词	音标	词性	释义	单词	音标	词性	释义
pricey	/ˈpraɪsi/	adj.	昂贵的	self-driving tour		phr.	自驾游
medical insurance		phr.	医疗保险	get through to		phr.	联系到，打通电话
mineral	/ˈmɪnərəl/	n.	矿物质	fleece	/fliːs/	v.	骗取钱财，敲诈
commission	/kəˈmɪʃn/	n.	佣金	reliable	/rɪˈlaɪəbl/	adj.	可信赖的
stick to		phr.	坚持，忠于	unlimited mileage		phr.	无里程限制，无限里程
fixed schedule		phr.	固定的时间表	seasonal promotion		phr.	季节性促销
bumpy	/ˈbʌmpi/	adj.	颠簸的	flag down		phr.	挥手拦下
pull over		phr.	靠路边停车	dispute over		phr.	就……争论

Part 3　　*Questions 21-30*

场景介绍

主题场景	课程作业	考查题型	选择题（多项）+ 笔记填空题
主旨大意	学生们讨论在研讨会上如何发表有关飞机引擎设计的演讲及怎样安排相关内容		

逐题精讲

Questions 21-23

　　题型：**选择题（多项）**

Questions 21-23

题目定位词 / 关键词	THREE things; include in their seminar presentation; quiz; lecture; slide presentation; short readings; group talk; group discussion; questions
录音原文定位	**WOMAN:** It might be better to ask questions. Otherwise, they may not suggest all the relevant ones. ... **WOMAN:** Then there has to be some direct input from us. **MAN:** Hm, but we should keep the lecture part brief... **WOMAN:** Well, will we have all of the information on slides, say?
题目解释	题干：选出三项学生们决定在研讨会演讲中包含的内容。 A：一个小测试 B：一个简短的讲座 C：幻灯片演示 D：一些阅读短文 E：小组谈话 F：小组讨论 G：一些问题 这道多选题要求找出学生们决定在他们的研讨会演讲中包含的三项内容。对话一开始男女同学就谈到了演讲的内容问题（But I have been thinking about the structure of the presentation），男同学提议让学生提问题，女同学则认为可能向他们提问更好，否则他们不会给建议（It might be better to ask questions. Otherwise, they may not suggest all the relevant ones）。随后，女同学提议直接说一些内容，男同学回答但需要保持讲座简短（keep the lecture part brief），而且要组织一些活动避免学生睡着。女同学建议小组讨论，男同学则建议让大家画设计图。最后，关于如何讲解清楚 main idea，男同学和女同学都同意将所有的信息放在幻灯片上（have all of the information on slides）。根据听力原文，考生会依次听到 ask questions、keep the lecture part brief 以及 slides，所以答案为选项 B、C、G，其中选项 B 中的 short 替换了原文中的 brief。
答案	ＢＣＧ（任意顺序）

Questions 24-30

题型：笔记填空题

Question 24

题目定位词 / 关键词	Seminar Outline; Establish problems; Concentrate on; problems
录音原文定位	And we should bring the focus specifically onto the environmental issues.
题目解释	第 24 至 30 题为笔记填空题，与研讨会的大纲有关。本题需要填写的内容与某个问题有关，该问题出现在 Establish problems 后面。女同学首先说 Well, first we need to establish what's wrong with the way things are at the moment, with regard to aircraft engine design，这部分内容就是 establish problems。之后女同学又补充说应该更加关注环保问题（we should bring the focus specifically onto the environmental issues），concentrate on 替换 bring the focus onto，答案就是 environmental。
答案	environmental

Question 25

题目定位词 / 关键词	Future situation; Production; decline
录音原文定位	WOMAN: So, after that, why don't we talk about the future situation? We need to stress that even when <u>petrol production begins to slow down in a few years,</u> it won't be the end of our problems, because there are alternatives like tar sands and, um, what's the other stuff?
题目解释	根据题干可知，第 25 题填写的内容属于 Future situation，听力原文从 why don't we talk about the future situation 开始讨论未来的情况。原文首先提到了汽油产量开始下降（petrol production begins to slow down），题干中的 decline 替换听力原文中的 slow down，所以这里需要填写的单词是 petrol。
答案	petrol

Question 26

题目定位词 / 关键词	Tar sands and oil shale; no
录音原文定位	WOMAN: So, after that, why don't we talk about the future situation? We need to stress that even when petrol production begins to slow down in a few years, it won't be the end of our problems, because there are alternatives like tar sands and, um, what's the other stuff? MAN: Oil shale? WOMAN: Right, oil shale. MAN: And <u>we really don't ever need to worry about either of those in terms of supply.</u> There are huge amounts available. Using them would mean that we could just go on using the same engines as we are now, and producing just as much pollution.

题目解释	根据题干可知，第26题有清晰的定位词tar sands and oil shale，比较容易在听力原文中找到对应的答案句。此外，空格前有否定词no，所以空格处应填写一个名词。根据这些关键信息可知，空格处需要填写的单词是supply，don't ever need to worry about either of those in terms of supply表示没有供应方面的问题。题干中的but produce pollution对应原文中的producing just as much pollution，据此也能确定答案。
答案	supply

Question 27

题目定位词/关键词	Alternative energy sources; hydrogen
录音原文定位	**WOMAN:** So then we need to put forward the safer alternative energy sources. **MAN:** And these need to be related to the two designs we're going to present later on. **WOMAN:** Yes, so there's the idea of using batteries instead of fuel-based engines. **MAN:** Yes, and there's hydrogen fuels.
题目解释	根据题干可知，第27题需要填写一种替代能源，其中之一的hydrogen（氢）已经给出。女同学说需要提出更安全的替代能源，然后提出了一个idea，即using batteries instead of fuel-based engines（使用电池代替燃油发动机），男同学则提出了hydrogen fuels，所以这里需要填写的单词是batteries。
答案	batteries

Question 28

题目定位词/关键词	Objections; too
录音原文定位	**MAN:** Umm... the next thing is probably to look at the problems we think will be identified with those alternatives. **WOMAN:** Yes. People are always worried about changing to totally new forms of technology. Well, I suppose that the first protest will be how expensive they are.
题目解释	根据题干可知，第28题与反对意见的第一条有关，同时因为too的存在，所以这个单词必须是形容词。男同学说the next thing is probably to look at the problems we think will be identified with those alternatives，意味着将开始讨论这些替代能源的问题。女同学首先提到人们总是担心换成全新的技术形式，第一个反对意见将是它们有多贵（the first protest will be how expensive they are）。根据这些内容可知，这里需要填写的单词是expensive。
答案	expensive

Question 29

题目定位词 / 关键词	difficult; generate power; and
录音原文定位	**MAN:** What other problems are there? **WOMAN:** Uh…I guess I'd have to say the next difficulty would be how to generate and store the power from those sources.
题目解释	根据题干可知，这里的内容属于反对意见的第二条，填写的单词是一个动词，逻辑上与 to generate power 并列。当听到 the next difficulty 时预示着答案即将出现，原文的 next difficulty 的内容是 how to generate and store the power from those sources，显然，与 generate 并列的是 store，因此答案就是 store。
答案	store

Question 30

题目定位词 / 关键词	not; design of present-day
录音原文定位	Because current engines are only designed to run on petroleum-based fuels.
题目解释	根据题干可知，这里的内容属于反对意见的第三条，填写的单词是一个名词。根据 design 和 present-day 两个关键词可以定位到听力原文 current engines are only designed to run on petroleum-based fuels，present-day 同义替换 current，名词 design 在原文中以动词形式 are only designed 出现，答案就是 engines。
答案	engines

场景词汇

单词	音标	词性	释义	单词	音标	词性	释义
seminar	/ˈsemɪnɑː(r)/	*n.*	研讨会	input	/ˈɪnpʊt/	*n.*	输入
structure	/ˈstrʌktʃə/	*n.*	结构	brief	/briːf/	*adj.*	简明的
associate	/əˈsəʊsieɪt/	*v.*	联系（常与 with 连用）	slide	/slaɪd/	*n.*	幻灯片
suggest	/səˈdʒest/	*v.*	提议，建议	protest	/ˈprəʊtest/	*n.*	反对，抗议
relevant	/ˈreləvənt/	*adj.*	相关的				

拓展词汇 |

单词	音标	词性	释义	单词	音标	词性	释义
aircraft	/ˈeəkrɑːft/	n.	飞机	engine	/ˈendʒɪn/	n.	引擎
supply	/səˈplaɪ/	n.	供给，供应	jot down		phr.	匆匆记下
alternative	/ɔːlˈtɜːnətɪv/	adj./ n.	可替代的 / 可供选择的事物，替代物	fuel-based engine		phr.	燃油发动机
bring the focus specifically onto		phr.	将注意力集中在	hydrogen	/ˈhaɪdrɪdʒən/	n.	氢，氢气
petrol	/ˈpetrəl/	n.	汽油	generate	/ˈdʒenəreɪt/	v.	生成

Part 4　　*Questions 31-40*

场景介绍

主题场景	人文社科	考查题型	选择题（单项）+ 配对题 + 表格填空题
主旨大意	一位女士在演讲中介绍了一位美国摄影师及这位摄影师出版的书籍		

逐题精讲

Questions 31-33

题型：选择题（单项）

Question 31

题目定位词 / 关键词	research Feininger's work; because; admired; took some well-known photographs; famous as both architect and photographer
录音原文定位	I decided I wanted to learn more about him when I recently saw his photographs of New York. <u>Some of them are really familiar, because you see them a lot on posters.</u>
题目解释	题干：学生选择研究 Feininger 的作品是因为什么？ A：她一直很欣赏他的照片 B：他拍摄了一些著名的关于纽约的照片 C：他作为建筑师和摄影师都很有名 本题问为何会选择研究 Feininger 的作品。在演讲者介绍完背景知识后，就提到了原因，她说最近看到 Feininger 拍摄的关于纽约的照片，对其中的一些很熟悉，因为常常在海报上看到它们。根据这一信息，选项中只有 B 符合要求。选项 A 的内容在听力原文中没有直接体现。选项 C 与原文不符，原文只说 he trained as an architect before becoming a photographer（他在成为摄影师之前接受过建筑师培训），但没有说他作为一个建筑师是有名的。
答案	B

Question 32

题目定位词 / 关键词	different; reality of life; cities look more beautiful; buildings from new angles
录音原文定位	But what really made him stand out from other photographers was his fascination with the idea of photographing—not just the beauty of cities, but showing them as a living, dynamic organism, sometimes even violent, with all their confusion and even their ugliness.

题目解释	题干：Feininger 的作品与其他摄影师有何不同？ A：他展示了生活的真实 B：他使城市看起来更漂亮 C：他以新的角度拍摄建筑物 当听力原文提到 what really made him stand out from other photographers 时意味着将要开始谈论他的与众不同之处，题干中的 different from 同义替换原文中的 stand out from。was 后面的内容解释了他的与众不同，即他对摄影想法的痴迷（his fascination with the idea of photographing）。由于这个说法有点抽象，演讲者又做了补充，即不仅要展示城市的美丽，而且要把它们作为一个有生命的、有活力的有机体，有时甚至是暴力的，包括它们所有的困惑甚至丑陋（not just the beauty of cities, but showing them as a living, dynamic organism, sometimes even violent, with all their confusion and even their ugliness）。根据这些表述，选项中只有 A 符合要求，它概括了演讲者所说的内容。选项 B 与听力原文的意思相左，摄影师不仅仅是把城市拍摄得更美丽，还有其他与众不同之处，注意 not just...but... 这个结构，转折词后的内容是重点强调内容。选项 C 在原文中没有涉及。
答案	A

Question 33

题目定位词 / 关键词	left *Life* magazine because; take different kinds of photographs; publish; travel
录音原文定位	Although he loved his work for *Life* magazine and had many opportunities to travel, he left in 1962 because he was eager to produce books of his photographs and techniques.
题目解释	题干：Feininger 离开《生活》杂志是因为他想做什么？ A：拍摄不同类型的照片 B：出版自己的思想和照片 C：有更多的旅行机会 本题问 Feininger 离开《生活》杂志的原因。根据关键词很容易定位到听力原文 he left in 1962 because... 这里提到他离职的原因是他渴望出版有关他照片和技术的书籍（he was eager to produce books of his photographs and techniques）。根据这些内容，选项中只有 B 与原文意思一致。选项 A 与听力原文相左，演讲中随后提到 he continued to take photos of urban scenes（他继续拍摄城市风光）。选项 C 的内容与原文不符，在《生活》杂志工作时他就有很多旅行机会了。
答案	B

Questions 34-36

题型：配对题

Question 34

题目定位词 / 关键词	1955
录音原文定位	The first major photographic exhibition to include his work took place in 1955 at the Museum of Modern Art, when Feininger was one of the several photographers represented in an exhibition called The Family of Man.
题目解释	根据题干可知，这道题是要匹配 1955 年展览的内容。根据时间很容易定位到原文。关于这一年的展览，听力原文中提到 when Feininger was one of the several photographers represented in an exhibition（当时 Feininger 是展览的几个摄影师之一），对应选项 E "与其他摄影师一起举办的展览"。
答案	E

Question 35

题目定位词 / 关键词	1957
录音原文定位	Two years later, in 1957, he had a solo exhibition of his nature themed works, which, for the first time, were mainly taken in color.
题目解释	同样地，根据时间 1957 年定位。原文中提到他举办了一个以自然为主题的个展（a solo exhibition of his nature themed works），选项只有选项 B "一场专注于自然的摄影展"符合原文内容。
答案	B

Question 36

题目定位词 / 关键词	1977
录音原文定位	The largest of these was in 1977, which was a retrospective exhibition of the International Center of Photography, bringing together photos taken at different stages of his life.
题目解释	原文提到 1977 年这个时间点时，说他举办了一次回顾展（a retrospective exhibition），汇集了他生命中不同阶段拍摄的照片（bringing together photos taken at different stages of his life），选项中只有选项 C "一场展示了他的职业发展的展览"符合原文内容。
答案	C

Test 3 解析

Questions 37-40

题型：表格填空题

Question 37

题目定位词 / 关键词	*New York in the Forties*; Buildings in the city; Good examples
录音原文定位	The first one is called *New York in the Forties*, so that tells you what it's about. Most of the photos are of buildings in the city, and they clearly show the methods he was so well known for.
题目解释	根据题干可知，这道题与书籍 *New York in the Forties* 有关，书籍主题是城市中的建筑，需要填写的内容在评价部分。听力原文中提到 they clearly show the methods he was so well known for（它们清楚地展示了他那出名的技巧），题干中的 Good examples 同义替换原文中的 he was so well known for，所以空格处需要填写 methods。
答案	methods

Question 38

题目定位词 / 关键词	*America Yesterday*; Every photograph was taken
录音原文定位	The second one's title is *America Yesterday*. It covers the 1940s to 1960s, and most of the photos are urban. Unlike some of his other books though, the photos aren't just of the center of American cities, but the suburbs too and their industries. It includes the famous 1942 Midtown Manhattan shot, taken from 25 miles away. In fact, all of the subjects in this book were photographed outdoors, and there are some wonderful ideas in this book that can help us improve our own photographs.
题目解释	根据题干可知，这道题与书籍 *America Yesterday* 有关，填写的内容涉及书籍的主题。首先，city centres, suburbs and industrial areas 已经在题干中出现了，需要填写的单词应与每张照片的拍摄有关，再结合语法知识，这个单词可能和地点、方位有关，是个副词。综合这些信息，听力原文中只有 outdoors 符合要求，photographed 与 taken 同义替换，all of the subjects 与 every photograph 同义替换。
答案	outdoors

Question 39

题目定位词 / 关键词	use; in photography
录音原文定位	...and there are some wonderful ideas in this book that can help us improve our own photographs. For example, Feininger always shows great understanding of the importance of light, and that's clearly displayed in this collection of photos.

题目解释	本题仍与书籍 *America Yesterday* 有关，需填写的内容是书籍的评价部分。题干的意思是这本书里有怎样在摄影中使用某个东西或某种技能的信息。本题紧跟上一题后，原文说这本书里有一些能帮助我们改进自己的照片的 ideas，ideas 对应题干中的 information，接着用 For example 举例说明 ideas 有什么。例子说的是 Feininger 对光的重要性的理解（great understanding of the importance of light），这在他的作品里有所体现，所以 light 符合要求。
答案	light

Question 40

题目定位词 / 关键词	*That's Photography*; Contains two
录音原文定位	The third book, *That's Photography*, is a collection of photographs of different places and eras, and contains many of his most famous ones. But it has a couple of essays which gave me a fascinating insight into his approach to photography.
题目解释	根据题干可知，这道题与书籍 *That's Photography* 有关，填写的内容是书籍的评价部分。空格前的数字 two 是一个重要信息，说明空格处是一个复数名词。根据这些信息，听力原文中只有 essays 符合要求，题干中的 two 同义替换原文中的 a couple of，contains 同义替换原文中的 has。
答案	essays

場景詞匯 |

单词	音标	词性	释义	单词	音标	词性	释义
architect	/ˈɑːkɪtekt/	n.	建筑师	collection	/kəˈlekʃn/	n.	收藏
pursue	/pəˈsjuː/	v.	追求	gallery	/ˈgæləri/	n.	陈列室；画廊
assignment	/əˈsaɪnmənt/	n.	任务	method	/ˈmeθəd/	n.	方法，措施
represent	/ˌreprɪˈzent/	v.	代表，展示	display	/dɪsˈpleɪ/	v.	陈列，展示
exhibition	/ˌeksɪˈbɪʃn/	n.	展览	insight	/ˈɪnsaɪt/	n.	洞察力

拓展词汇 |

单词	音标	词性	释义	单词	音标	词性	释义
stand out		*phr.*	脱颖而出	eager	/ˈiːgə/	*adj.*	渴望的
fascination	/ˌfæsɪˈneɪʃən/	*n.*	迷恋，入迷	solo	/ˈsəʊləʊ/	*adj.*	单独的
living	/ˈlɪvɪŋ/	*adj.*	活的	dynamic	/daɪˈnæmɪk/	*adj.*	充满活力的，动态的
organism	/ˈɔːgənɪzəm/	*n.*	有机体	retrospective	/ˌretrəˈspektɪv/	*adj.*	回顾的
violent	/ˈvaɪələnt/	*adj.*	暴力的	urban	/ˈɜːbən/	*adj.*	城市的
confusion	/kənˈfjuːʒən/	*n.*	困惑	suburb	/ˈsʌbɜːb/	*n.*	郊区
ugliness	/ˈʌglɪnɪs/	*n.*	丑陋	fascinating	/ˈfæsɪneɪtɪŋ/	*adj.*	极有吸引力的

Test 4 解析

Part 1　*Questions 1-10*

场景介绍

主题场景	活动介绍	考查题型	表格填空题
主旨大意	父亲和保姆一起为孩子制订一周的行程计划		

逐题精讲

题型：**表格填空题**

Question 1

题目定位词 / 关键词	Cost; online
录音原文定位	**Nanny:** Oh no, no, no, actually a ticket won't cost 10 pounds at all. During the holiday, it only sells at a price of £9.15. And if you book online in advance, it's even cheaper. You only need to pay £8.25 for each ticket.
题目解释	根据题干可知，空格处应填在线上买电影票的价格，答案应为数字。录音中提到了 9.15 英镑，但是是指在线下购买电影票的价格，在网上购买电影票只需要 8.25 英镑。
答案	8.25

Question 2

题目定位词 / 关键词	Bring
录音原文定位	**Nanny:** Yeah, sugar might be bad for her teeth. Why not bring her some water? **Father:** Water is great! Alright, then it's settled. What about Tuesday?
题目解释	根据题干可知，空格处应填给 Lily 带的东西，答案应为名词。录音中提到要给 Lily 带些喝的，但是不能带像果汁一样含糖的饮品，随后两人达成一致，认为带水最合适。
答案	water

Question 3

题目定位词 / 关键词	Tue.; Activity; family
录音原文定位	**Nanny:** Umm, why don't we have some outdoor activities on Tuesday? **Father:** Great idea! I know our community has organised a walk for families on that day, so you can go out for a walk together and get some fresh air.
题目解释	根据题干可知，空格处应填星期二进行的活动，答案应为名词。录音中保姆提议做一些户外运动，随后父亲想起周二社区组织了家庭散步活动，题干中的 family 以复数形式 families 在原文中出现，即可确认答案。
答案	walk

Question 4

题目定位词 / 关键词	Location
录音原文定位	**Father:** They used to carry out the activity in the Central Square, but now they've moved to the woods.
题目解释	根据题干可知，空格处应填周二活动的地点，答案应为地点名词。录音中提到原本这个活动在中央广场举办，现在移到了树林里，即可得出答案。
答案	woods

Question 5

题目定位词 / 关键词	Arrive; a.m.
录音原文定位	**Nanny:** I see. We'd better get there at 10:00 a.m., so we'll have to leave at 9:00 just in case.
题目解释	根据题干可知，空格处应填周二活动到达的时间，答案应为数字。录音中提到应该 10 点到达，get there 同义替换 arrive at，即可得出答案。后续提到 9 点，但是那是出发时间，与题干不符。
答案	10/10:00

Question 6

题目定位词 / 关键词	Bring
录音原文定位	**Father:** Right, another thing. There have been frequent showers recently, so the paths could be muddy that day. You might need to take Lily's boots with you.
题目解释	根据题干可知，空格处应填给 Lily 带去的东西，答案应为物品名词。bring 同义替换 take，即可得出答案。
答案	boots

Question 7

题目定位词 / 关键词	Wed.; Party; Lily's
录音原文定位	**Father:** Okay, now let's talk about what to do on Wednesday. Oh, her cousin has invited her to his party that day. I'm sure the kids will have a good time together.
题目解释	根据题干可知，空格处可填周三的派对是为了什么举办的，答案应为名词。通过 Wednesday 定位，是 Lily 的 cousin 邀请她参加派对的，即可得出这个派对是为 cousin 举办的。
答案	cousin

Question 8

题目定位词 / 关键词	Location; High Street
录音原文定位	**Nanny:** That's great. Where will the party be held? **Father:** The original plan was to have the party at the amusement park, but in the end they changed the location to High Street. There is a Japanese restaurant that the kids really love.
题目解释	根据题干可知，空格处应填周三派对的举办地点，答案应为与地点相关的单数可数名词。录音中先提到 amusement park，但是又改变了地址，题干中的关键词 High Street 原词重现，最终位置定为这条街上的一家日式餐馆，即可得出答案。
答案	restaurant

Question 9

题目定位词 / 关键词	Don't forget to
录音原文定位	**Father:** Oh, yes, yes. I almost forgot about that. The lesson should go on as planned. Take her to Huskey Hall. The lesson starts at 2 o'clock in the afternoon. And you have to pay for the fees at the end of each lesson. Make sure you've got enough money with you.
题目解释	根据题干可知，空格处应填周四活动不要忘记做的事情，to 后面填动词原形。本题前两项信息 music lesson 和 Huskey Hall 出现后，可知马上要提到与本题相关的内容。have to 同义替换 don't forget to，即可得出答案。
答案	pay

Question 10

题目定位词 / 关键词	laundry; Buy
录音原文定位	**Father:** And I remember there is a post office near the laundry. It'd be really nice of you if you could also buy some stamps for me. We're running out of them at home.
题目解释	根据题干可知，空格处应填需要活动后去买的东西，答案应为名词。录音中关键词 laundry 出现后，buy some 原词重现，即可得出答案。
答案	stamps

场景词汇

单词	音标	词性	释义	单词	音标	词性	释义
adventure movie		*phr.*	探险片	come up with		*phr.*	提出，想出
community	/kəˈmjuːnəti/	*n.*	社区	take place		*phr.*	发生；举行
boot	/buːt/	*n.*	靴子	amusement	/əˈmjuːzmənt/	*n.*	开心，娱乐
calendar	/ˈkælɪndə(r)/	*n.*	日历；日程表	hall	/hɔːl/	*n.*	礼堂，大厅
storytelling	/ˈstɔːritelɪŋ/	*n.*	讲故事	laundry	/ˈlɔːndri/	*n.*	要洗或已经洗好的衣物

拓展词汇

单词	音标	词性	释义	单词	音标	词性	释义
coupon	/ˈkuːpɒn/	*n.*	优惠券	shower	/ˈʃaʊə(r)/	*n.*	阵雨，阵雪
muddy	/ˈmʌdi/	*adj.*	泥泞的，多泥的	notebook	/ˈnəʊtbʊk/	*n.*	笔记本
pick up		*phr.*	拾取	run out of		*phr.*	用完

Part 2　*Questions 11-20*

场景介绍

主题场景	自然环境	考查题型	选择题（单项）+ 配对题
主旨大意	介绍一个新西兰的环境保护项目		

逐题精讲

Questions 11-15

　　题型：选择题（单项）

Question 11

题目定位词 / 关键词	highest risk
录音原文定位	**MAN:** ... The sea water, on the contrary, suffers from having a substantially lower quality due to human activities. You can see lots of bottles and plastic bags thrown around on beaches, which may later be swept into the sea, together with industrial waste water from the urban areas, causing pollution to the marine environment.
题目解释	题干：哪类环境现在最危险？ A：沙滩和海洋 B：高山和丘陵 C：河流和湖泊 录音中提到海水由于人类活动，质量变得越来越差，并列举了一系列表现，对应选项 A。原文中并未提及高山和丘陵的环境情况，故排除选项 B。录音中的 The first one is fresh water, such as streams in mountains or lakes in parks ...few issues have been reported concerning water quality 证明河流和湖泊的环境问题并不严重，故排除选项 C。
答案	A

Question 12

题目定位词 / 关键词	special; Project Tiri
录音原文定位	**MAN:** ... The unique vision of this project was to build an 'open sanctuary' for wildlife, which placed people at the heart of the project by allowing the public to be involved in the creation and evolution of this sanctuary.
题目解释	题干：Tiri 这个项目的特别之处是什么？ A：它对公众开放 B：只能种植本地植物 C：这是由志愿者种植的首个森林 通过 special 的同义替换词 unique 定位到听力原文，The unique vision of... 表明这个项目允许公众参与保护区的创建和发展，对应选项 A。录音中说志愿者们种植了来自 Matangi 及其附近岛屿的种子（with seeds sourced from Tiritiri Matangi and nearby islands），与选项 B 矛盾，故可排除。录音中只提到在 120 年的农耕后几乎没有了森林（was almost completely bare of forest following 120 years of farming），并未提及选项 C 中的内容，故可排除。
答案	A

Question 13

题目定位词 / 关键词	volunteers; doing
录音原文定位	**MAN:** ...so you can probably get a view of what the volunteers will be doing here: instead of revegetation like in the past, now they will get a chance to be involved in real research studies in the field, including species conservation, biodiversity monitoring, and invasive species management, furthering their science skills.
题目解释	题干：这个项目的志愿者们现在在做什么？ A：科学研究 B：种植树木 C：带队旅游 根据题干的要求，当听到原文 so you can probably get a view of what the volunteers will be doing here 时可预测答案即将出现。录音中表明现在他们能够参加真正的科学研究（be involved in real research studies），对应选项 A。植树是志愿者们过去做的事情（revegetation like in the past），而现在情况已经有所变化，故排除选项 B。这个岛是对外开放参观的，但是并不是志愿者们在做的事情，故排除选项 C。
答案	A

Question 14

题目定位词 / 关键词	most important; gain
录音原文定位	**MAN:** ...the biggest bonus of this volunteering experience is that they get to be a part of a wonderful team of excellent people from around the world. They will learn how to cooperate and strive for the same goal.
题目解释	题干：根据演讲者所述，志愿者们能从项目中得到的最重要的东西是什么？ A：教育效益 B：团队合作意识 C：身体健康 听力原文中的 the biggest bonus 同义替换题干中的 the most important thing，is 后面的表语从句即为具体内容。录音中表示这种志愿服务经历最大的好处是，他们可以成为一个由来自世界各地的优秀人才组成的优秀团队的一员（a part of a wonderful team of excellent people from around the world），他们将学会如何合作（learn how to cooperate），为同一个目标而努力（strive for the same goal），对应选项 B。选项 A、C 均有所提及（Apart from being a plus while applying for universities; enabled them to lose a few pounds），但都不是在这个项目里最重要的收获，故排除。
答案	B

Question 15

题目定位词 / 关键词	bring
录音原文定位	**MAN:** Well, there are all the equipment you might need on the island, so you don't have to worry about that. And the tap water is drinkable there, so no need to bring anything to drink either. You may need to bring some food in case you get hungry during the work.
题目解释	题干：志愿者们应该带什么去岛上？ A：饮品 B：工具 C：食物 女士问如果要去做志愿者需要带什么东西，男士的回答即为答案。男士说应该带些吃的，以防在工作中饿了，对应选项 C。选项 A、B 岛上会提供，不需要带去，故排除。
答案	C

Questions 16-20

题型：配对题

Question 16

题目定位词 / 关键词	Great Mercury Island
录音原文定位	**MAN:** ...For example, on the Great Mercury Island, you will help with the bioresearch and monitoring work. Besides using some special underwater equipment to observe the marine creatures and plants, you can also get into the water to have a closer look at the mysterious ocean yourself.
题目解释	本题通过项目名称定位，当听到 For example, on the Great Mercury Island 时预示答案即将出现。录音中说在工作过程中会使用一些特殊的水下设备来观察海洋生物和植物，还可以自己潜入水中，近距离观察海洋，对应选项 D"在水下工作"。
答案	D

Question 17

题目定位词 / 关键词	Treasure Island
录音原文定位	**MAN:** Then there is the Treasure Island project, in which you can participate in the heritage restoration. You will be given a tour around the ancient buildings and even help with their renovation.
题目解释	本题通过项目名称定位，当听到 Then there is the Treasure Island project 时预示答案即将出现。录音中说在这个项目中有机会参观古老的建筑，甚至可以帮助进行翻修，对应选项 E"修复建筑物"。
答案	E

Question 18

题目定位词 / 关键词	Coal Island
录音原文定位	**MAN:** The Coal Island is a very popular destination, too. Surrounded by mountains, it's a successful natural reserve home to many rare species. Here you can take a hike deep into the mountains and get in touch with nature.
题目解释	本题通过项目名称定位，当听到 The Coal Island is a very popular destination 时预示答案即将出现。录音中表示在这个项目中可以到深山中徒步，与自然接触，对应选项 A"爬山"。
答案	A

Question 19

题目定位词 / 关键词	The Waikite Valley
录音原文定位	**MAN:** Oh, I also recommend the Waikite Valley. The Department of Conservation has committed a lot of resources into restoring vulnerable species in the valley after grazing animals significantly damaged the area. So, as a volunteer, you can take part in the huge revegetation movement.
题目解释	本题通过项目名称定位，当听到 I also recommend the Waikite Valley 时预示答案即将出现。录音中表示作为一名志愿者，可以参与到大规模的植被重建运动中来，对应选项 G "种植植物"。
答案	G

Question 20

题目定位词 / 关键词	Tuatapere Hump Ridge
录音原文定位	**MAN:** Tuatapera Hump Ridge is another interesting place to go... Sign up to be a volunteer, and you can get the opportunity to have hands-on experience of track construction and repair.
题目解释	本题通过项目名称定位，当听到 Tuatapera Hump Ridge is another interesting place to go 时预示答案即将出现。录音中表示在这个项目中做志愿者，就有机会实际体验轨道建设和维修，对应选项 F "修建道路"。
答案	F

Test 4 解析

场景词汇

单词	音标	词性	释义	单词	音标	词性	释义
shed light on		*phr.*	阐明	sustainable	/səˈsteɪnəbl/	*adj.*	可持续的
stream	/striːm/	*n.*	小河，小溪	flourish	/ˈflʌrɪʃ/	*v.*	（植物或动物）长势好
substantially	/səbˈstænʃəli/	*adv.*	大量地，可观地	urban	/ˈɜːbən/	*adj.*	城市的，城镇的
marine	/məˈriːn/	*adj.*	海洋的	enact	/ɪˈnækt/	*v.*	制定，通过，颁布
awareness	/əˈweənəs/	*n.*	认识，意识	conservation	/ˌkɒnsəˈveɪʃn/	*n.*	保护，保存
biodiversity	/ˌbaɪəʊdaɪˈvɜːsəti/	*n.*	生物多样性	restoration	/ˌrestəˈreɪʃn/	*n.*	修复，恢复

拓展词汇 |

单词	音标	词性	释义	单词	音标	词性	释义
contrary	/ˈkɒntrəri/	adj.	相反的，相对的	suffer from		phr.	忍受，遭受
arrest	/əˈrest/	v.	阻止，抑制	sanctuary	/ˈsæŋktʃuəri/	n.	庇护所，保护区
underpin	/ˌʌndəˈpɪn/	v.	支持，巩固	revegetation	/ˌriːˌvedʒiˈteɪʃn/	n.	再种植；再生长
invasive	/ɪnˈveɪsɪv/	adj.	侵入的	testimonial	/ˌtestɪˈməʊniəl/	n.	证明书；推荐书
strive for		phr.	努力，力争	tempting	/ˈtemptɪŋ/	adj.	诱人的，吸引人的
retrieve	/rɪˈtriːv/	v.	找回，收回	renovation	/ˌrenəˈveɪʃn/	n.	翻新，整修

Part 3　　*Questions 21-30*

场景介绍 |

主题场景	课程作业	考查题型	选择题（单项）+ 配对题
主旨大意	学生和导师讨论关于双语学习对婴儿的影响		

逐题精讲 |

Questions 21-25

　　题型：选择题（单项）

Question 21

题目定位词 / 关键词	Brian; trouble
录音原文定位	**TUTOR:** That's good. What's the problem, then? **STUDENT:** Well, I've narrowed down my research to one specific area, but I'm currently struggling over how to put my thoughts together into a well-organized paper.
题目解释	题干：Brian 在写论文的过程中碰到了什么问题？ A：寻找足够的信息 B：组织内容 C：专注某一个领域 定位时，原文中的 problem 同义替换题干中的 trouble。学生表示自己现在正在努力把想法整理成一篇条理清晰的论文，put thoughts together 同义替换 structuring，对应选项 B。选项 A、C 在文中都有所提及（it's not hard to gather the information I need；I've narrowed down my research to one specific area），但都不是学生遇到的问题，故均排除。
答案	B

Question 22

题目定位词 / 关键词	Why; choose
录音原文定位	**STUDENT:** It's true that not many have, but it doesn't influence me. Actually, this area aroused my interest when I discovered that critics had changed their tune regarding bilingualism as time went by. So, I wanted to investigate what effects it will really have on children.

题目解释	题干：Brian 为什么选择这个话题？ A：人们对双语学习的态度有所改变 B：他一直对这个话题很感兴趣 C：选这个话题的学生不多 导师问 could you tell me why you decided to study this topic in the first place，预示答案即将出现。学生表示因为发现批评家们对双语的态度发生了变化，所以才对这个话题感兴趣，对应选项 A。学生表示他一开始对这个话题是很反感的（at first I was also put off by this topic），与选项 B 矛盾，故排除。选项 C 在文中有所提及，但是这并非影响学生做决定的因素（It's true that not many have, but it doesn't influence me），故排除。
答案	A

Question 23

题目定位词 / 关键词	negative belief; originally
录音原文定位	STUDENT: The truth was, back then, it was commonly believed that learning two languages simultaneously could easily confuse children.
题目解释	题干：人们原先对双语教学有什么消极的看法？ A：双语孩子比同龄人开始说话晚 B：双语孩子常常混淆两种语言 C：双语孩子的任何一门语言都比不上以这些语言为母语的人 导师问 Why did they think poorly of bilingual education in the past，预示答案即将出现。学生说人们认为同时学习两门语言容易使孩子感到困惑，confuse 同义替换 mix up，对应选项 B。原文中提到了选项 A 中所说的学习双语的孩子说话晚（recent evidence also reveals that bilingual children might not be able to start speaking either of their languages when other monolingual kids have already begun），但是这是现在的研究，并不是人们原来对双语学习的看法，故排除。选项 C 所说的双语孩子的任何一门语言都比不上以这些语言为母语的人也在文中有所提及，但是后续被否定了（children's proficiency in either of the languages will never match up with the level of monolingual native speakers. However, that was not the real reason... ），故排除。
答案	B

Question 24

题目定位词 / 关键词	agree; biggest advantage
录音原文定位	STUDENT: Mm... You're right. Since the child has to cope with two different languages at a time, it's been proven that their multi-tasking ability will be stronger than others'.

题目解释	题干：导师和 Brian 都赞成双语学习最大的好处是什么？ A：他们更有可能在将来获得更好的就业机会 B：他们常常在学校表现优秀 C：他们更能同时处理几项任务 当学生说 people have come to realise the benefits of bilingualism 时预示答案即将出现。学生表示由于他们需要同时学习两门语言，所以多任务处理能力会更好，multi-tasking 同义替换 dealing with several tasks at the same time，对应选项 C。这个话题下学生首先提到掌握两门语言能够找到更好的工作 (they assume that mastering several languages will help them get a better job when they grow up)，对应选项 A，但是导师认为这只是部分人认为的，并不一定是这样的 (is not necessarily the case)，所以排除选项 A。随后学生又提到双语学习的孩子注意力更集中，在学校更容易取得好成绩 (performed better on attention tests and had better concentration compared)，对应选项 B，但是导师仍然不认为这是最主要的 (that's still not the most essential skill)，所以排除选项 B。
答案	C

Question 25

题目定位词 / 关键词	biggest challenge; parents
录音原文定位	STUDENT: Right, due to these advantages, many parents are now making efforts to cultivate their kids' bilingual ability. To meet the market's demand, there are also lots of bilingual learning institutes out there. But the biggest problem is it can be rather costly for parents.
题目解释	题干：双语学习孩子的家长们面临的最大挑战是什么？ A：寻找双语学校 B：培养双语兴趣 C：负担双语教育的费用 通过 many parents are now making efforts to cultivate their kids' bilingual ability 可知，话题转向家长，预示答案即将出现。biggest problem 同义替换 biggest challenge，costly 同义替换 affording the fees，对应选项 C。原文中提到市面上有许多双语机构 (there are also lots of bilingual learning institutes)，所以排除选项 A。原文中提到家长们愿意为双语学习的孩子们报课外班 (parents also like to take their kids to some extracurricular bilingual activities)，故这并不是家长们面临的问题，排除选项 B。
答案	C

Test 4 解析

Questions 26-30

题型：**配对题**

Question 26

题目定位词 / 关键词	Richard Floridi
录音原文定位	**STUDENT:** I've already read a wide range of research in this field. Richard Floridi was one of the pioneers who realised the significance of bilingualism on children's development, so he tracked the lives of some bilingual children to find out its long-term effects on them. **TUTOR:** Definitely. His work was ground-breaking but due to limited conditions at that time, he couldn't gather enough volunteers so there were not enough samples to support his conclusions.
题目解释	本题通过人名定位，当听到 Richard Floridi was one of the pioneers who realised 时预示答案即将出现。原文中的 couldn't gather enough volunteers 和 not enough samples 同义替换 had too few research participants，对应选项 A"研究对象太少了"。
答案	A

Question 27

题目定位词 / 关键词	Prof. Woodcock
录音原文定位	**STUDENT:** Yes, that's a real pity, but his work has inspired many later researchers. For example, Professor Woodcock, from the University of Southampton, enlarged the sample size and furthered his studies. **TUTOR:** Right, although he'd got enough data, the sources of it were not very reliable. Instead of participating in the investigation himself, he just collected those bilingual children's cases from different places and he failed to carry out an in-depth analysis of the materials.
题目解释	本题通过人名定位，当听到 For example, Professor Woodcock, from the University of Southampton 时预示答案即将出现。导师说他没能够对材料进行深度分析，与选项 D"数据分析很差"相对应。
答案	D

Question 28

题目定位词 / 关键词	Prof. Granger
录音原文定位	STUDENT: I see... I also read Professor Granger's research. She's one of the leading neuroscientists exploring how the brains of bilingual kids work. ... STUDENT: That's right. And she explained all her experiments in an elaborate way, including her hypothesis, methods, data collection, analysis and so on.
题目解释	本题通过人名定位，当听到 I also read Professor Granger's research 时预示答案即将出现。学生说她详细地解释了她所有的实验，in an elaborate way 同义替换 details，对应选项 F。
答案	F

Question 29

题目定位词 / 关键词	Prof. Brito
录音原文定位	TUTOR: Also, there is a professor named Brito whose work is on your must-read list. STUDENT: Oh really? What's special about his studies? TUTOR: He recorded the daily conversations of normal bilingual families and observed how the babies gradually built their vocabulary, mastered grammar and switched between different languages, and he did this using cutting-edge speech analysis equipment in his laboratory.
题目解释	本题通过人名定位，当听到 there is a professor named Brito whose work is on your must-read list 时预示答案即将出现。导师说他在实验室用了尖端的语音分析设备，cutting-edge equipment 同义替换 new technology，对应选项 B。
答案	B

Question 30

题目定位词 / 关键词	Maria Baralt
录音原文定位	TUTOR: Oh right, and the studies of Maria Baralt are also worth reading. Her research interest is how the growth of globalisation has motivated bilingual education in society, and she mainly focuses on America, a typical immigrant country.
题目解释	本题通过人名定位，当听到 and the studies of Maria Baralt are also worth reading 时预示答案即将出现。导师提到她的研究方向是全球化发展如何推动双语教育的发展，globalisation 同义替换 global，对应选项 E。
答案	E

Test 4 解析

场景词汇

单词	音标	词性	释义	单词	音标	词性	释义
bilingual	/ˌbaɪˈlɪŋgwəl/	adj.	能说两种语言的	narrow down		phr.	缩小；限制；减少；变窄
well-organized	/welˈɔːgənaizd/	adj.	有序的；很有条理的	investigate	/ɪnˈvestɪgeɪt/	v.	调查，研究
proficiency	/prəˈfɪʃnsi/	n.	熟练，精通	monolingual	/ˌmɒnəˈlɪŋgwəl/	adj.	单语的；仅用一种语言的
sceptical	/ˈskeptɪkl/	adj.	持怀疑态度的	reveal	/rɪˈviːl/	v.	揭示，透露
assume	/əˈsjuːm/	v.	假定，假设	cope with		phr.	处理，应付
elaborate	/ɪˈlæbərət/	adj.	详细的	hypothesis	/haɪˈpɒθəsɪs/	n.	假说，假设

拓展词汇

单词	音标	词性	释义	单词	音标	词性	释义
struggle	/ˈstrʌgl/	v.	奋力，努力	arouse	/əˈraʊz/	v.	引起，激起
critic	/ˈkrɪtɪk/	n.	批评者，评论员	simultaneously	/ˌsɪməlˈteɪniəsli/	adv.	同时地
confuse	/kənˈfjuːz/	v.	使糊涂，使困惑	toggle	/ˈtɒgl/	v.	切换，转换
back and forth		phr.	反复地，来回地	costly	/ˈkɒstli/	adj.	昂贵的，值钱的
track	/træk/	v.	轨道	ground-breaking	/ˈgraʊndbreɪkɪŋ/	adj.	独创的；开拓性的
neuroscientist	/ˈnjʊərəʊsaɪəntɪst/	n.	神经系统科学家	cutting-edge	/ˌkʌtɪŋ ˈedʒ/	adj.	领先的
immigrant	/ˈɪmɪgrənt/	adj.	移民的，迁入的				

Part 4　　*Questions 31-40*

场景介绍 |

主题场景	城市交通	考查题型	笔记填空题
主旨大意	城镇的现状以及未来的发展计划		

逐题精讲 |

题型：**笔记填空题**

Question 31

题目定位词 / 关键词	Traditionally; strong
录音原文定位	Decades ago, most citizens built up their fortune through the furniture business, which was the town's most well-known industry in the past.
题目解释	根据题干可以预判空格处应填这座城镇原来在哪个行业比较强，答案应为名词或形容词。当听到录音中出现本题前一项信息的关键词 population 和 16,000 时，预示即将进入与本题相关的内容。当听到录音中说十年前大多数市民都是通过家具业积累财富的，这在过去是镇上最知名的行业时，即可确定答案，decades ago 同义替换 traditionally，most well-known 替换 strong，答案为 furniture。
答案	furniture

Question 32

题目定位词 / 关键词	Now; fastest
录音原文定位	As time has gone by, the service sector has gradually risen to become the most important industry in this town, making up 2/3 of all the industries.
题目解释	根据题干可以预判空格处应填该城镇现在增长最快的部门，答案应为形容词或名词。当录音中提到 However, recent years have witnessed some transformations in the town's various industries 时预示话题即将从谈论过去的产业转变到谈论现在的产业。录音中说服务业逐渐上升为这个城镇最重要的产业，占所有产业的 2/3，most important 和 making up 2/3 同义替换 fastest developing，即可得出增长最快的是 service sector。
答案	service

Question 33

题目定位词 / 关键词	company; 600
录音原文定位	For example, financial services have been booming these years, and one big insurance company has hired 600 workers since its establishment.
题目解释	根据题干可以预判空格处应填某种公司类型，答案应为名词或形容词。根据数字 600 即可定位，录音中说一家大型保险公司自成立以来已经雇用了 600 名员工，one big company 同义替换 a major company，hired 600 workers 同义替换 employs 600 people，答案随即出现。
答案	insurance

Question 34

题目定位词 / 关键词	Road; near
录音原文定位	So, emphasis should be given to tackling congestion in these areas, especially near the schools in the centre of the town.
题目解释	根据题干可以预判空格处应填交通较为繁忙的地段，答案应为与地点相关的名词。在听录音的过程中可以通过 road 定位到 Barningham is one of the most accessible places by road，预示答案即将出现。录音中提到应该重视解决这些地区的交通拥堵问题，特别是在市中心学校附近，congestion 同义替换 busy，near 原词重现，即可确定答案为 schools。注意，原文中的 London 为混淆项，原文指的是这座城市在伦敦附近，并不是指交通繁忙的地段。
答案	schools

Question 35

题目定位词 / 关键词	new homes; new
录音原文定位	What's more, more employment opportunities will be created to ensure the livelihood of the increasing population and to stimulate the economy. An estimate of 20,000 new jobs will be provided to the local residents.
题目解释	根据题干可以预判空格处应填这座城市新增加的项目，答案应为名词。根据本题前一项信息的关键词 homes 可以定位到 it will enlarge its residential area by establishing 16,000 new houses...to settle in，当听到 What's more 时预示与本题相关的内容即将出现。录音中提到将创造更多就业机会，预计将为当地居民提供 2 万个新工作岗位，new 原词重现，答案即可确认。注意，employment opportunities 也符合预判，但是答案要求为 ONE WORD ONLY，所以正确答案为 jobs。
答案	jobs

Test 4 解析

Question 36

题目定位词 / 关键词	new; university
录音原文定位	The university also plans to set up a new campus nearby to build more laboratories.
题目解释	根据题干可以预判空格处应填在大学周围新建的建筑，答案应为名词。通过本题前一项信息的关键词 scientific research park 和 university 可以定位到 The local university aims to establish a scientific and technological incubator to enhance its research ability，本句结束后，与本题相关的内容随即出现。录音中说该大学还计划在附近建立一个新校区，以建立更多的实验室，set up 同义替换 build，new 原词重现，nearby 同义替换 near，即可确定答案为 campus。
答案	campus

Question 37

题目定位词 / 关键词	Reduce; 20%
录音原文定位	The local government is making efforts to mitigate traffic flow by 20% through its five-year plan.
题目解释	根据题干可以预判空格处应填减少了 20% 的事物或现象，答案应为名词。本题可直接根据数字 20% 定位，录音中说当地政府正在努力通过五年计划将交通流量减少 20%，mitigate 同义替换 reduce，20% 这一关键词也原词重现，因字数要求，可确定答案为 traffic。
答案	traffic

Question 38

题目定位词 / 关键词	Encourage
录音原文定位	Instead, cycling, as an eco-friendly mode of transport, is strongly advocated, so...
题目解释	根据题干可以预判空格处应填城市中的某种现象或行为，答案应为名词。通过 For this purpose, private cars are discouraged on the roads 和 Instead 一词可知，后面即将提到受鼓励的行为。录音中说单车作为一种生态友好的交通方式将会被大力提倡，strongly advocated 同义替换 encourage，即可得出答案为 cycling。
答案	cycling

Question 39

题目定位词 / 关键词	Floor space; 10,000
录音原文定位	Increased investment from the government will allow the town to allocate 10,000 square metres to establish supermarkets, shopping malls and department stores, promoting the vitality of retail businesses.
题目解释	根据题干可以预判空格处应填 10,000 平方米空地的用途，答案应为名词。通过 10,000 square metres 定位到 Increased investment ... 10,000 square metres，预示答案即将出现。录音中说这 10,000 平方米的地会用来建超市、购物中心和百货公司，以提升零售业的活力，即可得出空地用于零售业。
答案	retail

Question 40

题目定位词 / 关键词	8,000
录音原文定位	Besides that, about 8,000 square metres have been designated for the construction of office areas...
题目解释	根据题干可以预判空格处应填 8,000 平方米空地的用途，答案应为名词。通过 8,000 可以定位到 about 8,000 square metres have been designated for the construction of office areas，由本句可知这些地是用来建造办公区的。
答案	office

场景词汇

单词	音标	词性	释义	单词	音标	词性	释义
turning point		phr.	转折点	emerge	/ɪˈmɜːdʒ/	v.	浮现，出现
perception	/pəˈsepʃn/	n.	看法，认识	commercial	/kəˈmɜːʃl/	adj.	商业的
fortune	/ˈfɔːtʃuːn/	n.	财富	boom	/buːm/	v.	迅速发展，繁荣
insurance	/ɪnˈʃʊərəns/	n.	保险，保险业	hire	/ˈhaɪə(r)/	v.	聘用，录用
tackle	/ˈtækl/	v.	应付，解决	congestion	/kənˈdʒestʃən/	n.	拥塞，塞车
residential	/ˌrezɪˈdenʃl/	adj.	住宅区的，居民区的	livelihood	/ˈlaɪvlihʊd/	n.	生计，营生
retail	/ˈriːteɪl/	n.	零售	skyscraper	/ˈskaɪskreɪpə(r)/	n.	摩天大楼

拓展词汇 |

单词	音标	词性	释义	单词	音标	词性	释义
craftsmanship	/ˈkrɑːftsmənʃɪp/	n.	手艺，工艺	competitiveness	/kəmˈpetətɪvnəs/	n.	竞争力
campaign	/kæmˈpeɪn/	v.	领导（参加）运动	stimulate	/ˈstɪmjuleɪt/	v.	促进，激发
incubator	/ˈɪŋkjubeɪtə(r)/	n.	孵化器	enhance	/ɪnˈhɑːns/	v.	增强，提高
accessibility	/əkˌsesəˈbɪləti/	n.	可及性，可达性	mitigate	/ˈmɪtɪgeɪt/	v.	减轻，缓和
advocate	/ˈædvəkeɪt/	v.	拥护，提倡	allocate	/ˈæləkeɪt/	v.	分配，分派

Test 4 解析

Test 5 解析

Part 1 *Questions 1-10*

场景介绍

主题场景	日常咨询		考查题型	笔记填空题
主旨大意	一位女士打电话咨询社区大学的各类课程信息			

逐题精讲

题型：**笔记填空题**

Question 1

题目定位词 / 关键词	beginners; starts at
录音原文定位	**WOMAN:** Sounds great! When does the class usually begin? **MAN:** Well, we have two separate schedules for different levels of students. <u>If you've never learned guitar before, the class begins at 7:45 in the morning</u>...
题目解释	根据题干中的 starts at 可知，空格处应填写课程开始的具体时间。当录音中女士问 When does the class usually begin 时预示答案即将出现，结合题干中的 beginners，可对应到录音中的 If you've never learned guitar before，即之前没学过吉他，也就是初学者，所以答案就在 the class begins at 7:45 in the morning 里，其中 in the morning 对应题干中的 a.m.，由此可知答案为 7:45。
答案	7:45

Question 2

题目定位词 / 关键词	something to; on
录音原文定位	**WOMAN:** Alright. Should I bring my own guitar to the class then? **MAN:** Yes, you should. <u>And you'd better bring something you can write on to take notes during the class</u>...
题目解释	根据题干可知，空格处应填关于吉他课需携带之物，答案应为动词原形，并且可以和 on 构成词组。当女士问 Should I bring my own guitar to the class then 时预示答案即将出现。录音中工作人员回答说 And you'd better bring something you can write on，由此可知答案为 write。
答案	write

Question 3

题目定位词 / 关键词	$
录音原文定位	**WOMAN:** You're right. I won't forget that. I also want to acquire some knowledge of first aid. I think that can be very important, especially when there's any emergency. Could you tell me more about this course? **MAN:** Absolutely! It's on Tuesday every week and it costs 140 dollars for 4 classes in total...
题目解释	根据题干中的 $ 可知，空格处应该填写 First Aid 课程的花费，录音中女士问 Could you tell me more about this course，工作人员回答 it costs 140 dollars，由此可知答案为 140。
答案	140

Question 4

题目定位词 / 关键词	extra; $; ingredients
录音原文定位	**MAN:** Well, yes, the course fee is still 60 dollars but you will also still need to pay an additional 56 dollars for the ingredients you will use during the class...
题目解释	根据题干可知，空格处应该填写 Asian Cooking 课程的费用，并需根据 extra 和 ingredients 去定位。录音中工作人员回答需要为食材额外花费 56 dollars，additional 对应题干中的 extra，由此可知答案为 56。
答案	56

Question 5

题目定位词 / 关键词	manual; and a
录音原文定位	**MAN:** At the beginning of the course, every student will be given a manual for free, and after you finish all the classes, you'll receive a certificate.
题目解释	根据题干可知，空格处应填入一个单数可数名词，并需根据 manual 去定位，关注与之并列的信息。录音中工作人员说所有学生都会得到一个免费的 manual，课程结束后还会得到一张 certificate，由此可知答案为 certificate。
答案	certificate

Test 5 解析

Question 6

题目定位词 / 关键词	containers; a
录音原文定位	**WOMAN:** I can't wait to begin. Oh, <u>I remember we have to bring a knife to the cooking class, right?</u> **MAN:** That's right. You also need to bring some bowls or plates for the seasonings or other ingredients.
题目解释	根据题干可知，空格处应填入一个单数可数名词，和 containers 同属于 Asian Cooking 课程所需携带之物。录音中女士提到 I remember we have to bring a knife to the cooking class, right? 紧接着工作人员回答 That's right. You also need to bring some bowls or plates，工作人员表示同意女士的说法，而 bowls or plates 对应题干中的 containers，由此可知答案为 knife。
答案	knife

Question 7

题目定位词 / 关键词	Good for; problems
录音原文定位	**WOMAN:** Right! I think some yoga moves would be good for her neck...
题目解释	根据题干可知，空格处应该填写 Yoga 课程给某些问题、疾病带来的好处。录音中女士提到 I think some yoga moves would be good for her neck，由此可知答案为 neck。
答案	neck

Question 8

题目定位词 / 关键词	Yoga; Need to bring
录音原文定位	**WOMAN:** Does she need to wear any special footwear for the class? **MAN:** No need at all. During the class, everyone does yoga on the floor so you don't even have to wear any shoes. **WOMAN:** Alright. <u>She will just bring a towel then.</u> She might also need a mat, but I suppose that's provided in the class? **MAN:** Yes. There is a special mat for all the students.
题目解释	本题空格前后无定位词，只能根据更大范围的 Yoga 和标题中的 need to bring 去定位，找出一个名词。录音中女士问是否需要携带 footwear，工作人员的回答是 No need at all（完全不需要），而当女士说 She will just bring a towel then 时，工作人员没有反对，由此可知答案为 towel。
答案	towel

Question 9

题目定位词 / 关键词	In; Community Centre
录音原文定位	**MAN**: Okay. We teach both day and night makeup and the class will be held in Lawnton Community Centre. **WOMAN**: Lawnton? Could you spell it out for me? **MAN**: L - A - W - N - T - O - N.
题目解释	根据题干可知，空格处应该填写 makeup 课程的地点，可以根据 Community Centre 去定位。录音中工作人员提到 the class will be held in Lawnton Community Centre，并在下文明确给出该地点的拼写 L - A - W - N - T - O - N，由此可知答案为 Lawnton。
答案	Lawnton

Question 10

题目定位词 / 关键词	brushes; a small
录音原文定位	**WOMAN**: Okay. Should she bring her own makeup or is it provided? **MAN**: Oh, all students should use their own makeup. Also, don't forget to ask her to bring some brushes and a small mirror.
题目解释	根据题干可知，空格处应该填入一个单数可数名词，而且和 brushes 同属于 makeup 课程所需携带之物。女士问需不需要自带化妆品，工作人员回答所有人都要自己带，而且还要带一些刷子和一把小镜子，由此可知答案为 mirror。
答案	mirror

场景词汇

单词	音标	词性	释义	单词	音标	词性	释义
course	/kɔːs/	n.	课程	fee	/fiː/	n.	费用
schedule	/ˈʃedjuːl/	n.	日程安排	take notes		phr.	记笔记
take in		phr.	吸收；领会	acquire	/əˈkwaɪə(r)/	v.	获得，学到
first aid		phr.	急救护理	cost	/kɒst/	v.	价钱为，需花费
advanced course		phr.	高级课程	qualification	/ˌkwɒlɪfɪˈkeɪʃn/	n.	资格，学历
manual	/ˈmænjuəl/	n.	使用手册	certificate	/səˈtɪfɪkət/	n.	证明，证书；文凭
recommend	/ˌrekəˈmend/	v.	推荐				

拓展词汇

单词	音标	词性	释义	单词	音标	词性	释义
a wide range of		*phr.*	多种多样的	particularly	/pəˈtɪkjələli/	*adv.*	非常，尤其
separate	/ˈseprət/	*adj.*	分开的；不同的	emergency	/ɪˈmɜːdʒənsi/	*n.*	突发事件，紧急情况
terrific	/təˈrɪfɪk/	*adj.*	极好的，了不起的	additional	/əˈdɪʃənl/	*adj.*	附加的，额外的
seasoning	/ˈsiːzənɪŋ/	*n.*	调味品	uniform	/ˈjuːnɪfɔːm/	*n.*	制服，校服
dress code		*phr.*	着装要求				

Part 2　　*Questions 11-20*

场景介绍

主题场景	人文社科	考查题型	选择题（单项）+ 流程图题
主旨大意	一位志愿者介绍在铁器时代风格的村庄生活以及制造圆木屋的流程		

逐题精讲

Questions 11-15

　　题型：选择题（单项）

Question 11

题目定位词 / 关键词	typical day; cold at night; gets up early; not have enough time
录音原文定位	WOMAN: ... So Jim, could you describe to us what a normal day was like in such an ancient village? MAN: Hi, guys. Well, I'd say the biggest difference is that I've come to get up really early every morning.
题目解释	题干：Jim 描述的村庄里典型的一天是什么样的？ A：他感觉晚上很冷 B：他总是起得很早 C：他没有足够的属于自己的时间 当听到女士提问 could you describe to us what a normal day was like 时，预示答案即将出现（normal 为 typical 的同义替换），Jim 回答最大的不同是每天要早起，由此可知答案为选项 B。选项 A 为下文提到的其他人对村庄生活的抱怨，但这对 Jim 来说不是问题（Some of them complained that it was because they couldn't sleep well due to the coldness at night, though that was not really a problem for me），故排除选项 A。选项 C 为原文 I could enjoy the "me time" for a while 的干扰信息，原文说的是以前早上醒来后可以享受一会儿私人专属时间，并不等同于现在没有自己的时间，故排除选项 C。
答案	B

Question 12

题目定位词 / 关键词	breakfast; takes time to prepare; hard to get used to; eating quickly
录音原文定位	MAN: That's true. After we got up, we would start making breakfast. Usually we had porridge and fruits. It might put some people off when they hear that, but in fact it tasted good and was healthy too. We usually started preparing the ingredients the night before and spent much effort cooking it in the morning. We got used to it and started liking it in no time. And we would all just gather around and slowly enjoy the meal.

题目解释	题干：Jim 关于村庄里早餐的描述是怎样的? A：需要花时间准备 B：很难习惯 C：人们很快就吃完了 由 breakfast 可定位至 we would start making breakfast，后文中 Jim 说通常会在前一天晚上开始准备食材，然后在第二天早上花很多精力烹饪，意味着准备早饭比较耗时，由此可知答案为选项 A。选项 B 与原文 in fact it tasted good and was healthy too（事实上味道还不错而且很健康）矛盾，故排除选项 B。选项 C 与原文 all just gather around and slowly enjoy the meal（聚在一起慢慢地享受早餐）矛盾，故排除选项 C。
答案	A

Question 13

题目定位词 / 关键词	evening meal; too tired; fruits and berries; talk about what they've done
录音原文定位	WOMAN: That sounds nice. What about your dinner? MAN: Well, normally dinner was supposed to be an occasion for people to gather around and share their day, but in the village, sometimes we were too exhausted after a whole day's work. So, we'd just skip the meal and go to bed.
题目解释	题干：村庄里的晚餐是怎样的? A：有时候人们太累了就不吃了 B：他们的主要食物是水果和浆果 C：人们常常讨论他们白天做了什么 当听到女士提问 What about your dinner 时，预示答案即将出现。Jim 回答有时一天的工作太累了，所以就跳过这顿饭不吃了，由此可知答案为选项 A，原文中的 exhausted 被 tired 替换了。选项 B 以偏概全，原文提到晚餐包括水果、浆果、坚果以及在树林里收集的各种东西（Most of the time we ate fruits, berries, nuts and all sorts of things we gathered in the woods），故排除选项 B。选项 C 看似在原文出现，但原文 normally dinner was supposed to be an occasion for people to gather around and share their day 说的是通常人们所认为的情况，并不符合该村庄的实际情况，故也排除。
答案	A

Question 14

题目定位词 / 关键词	the most important work; blacksmith; mend; maintain; collect
录音原文定位	MAN: For example, for a blacksmith, his main job was to make sure that the fire in the house kept burning so that people wouldn't suffer from coldness. It allowed people to carry out all the other tasks.
题目解释	题干：铁匠最重要的工作是什么？ A：修理工具和设备 B：维持稳定的热源 C：收集食物 由 blacksmith 可定位至 for a blacksmith, his main job was to make sure that the fire in the house kept burning，由此可知答案为选项 B，其中 maintain 对应原文中的 kept，一直燃烧的火就等于稳定的热源。选项 A 对应原文 the blacksmith was also responsible for repairing the broken tools and other equipment，虽然选项 A 也是 blacksmith 的职责，但不是 the most important work，故排除选项 A。选项 C collect food 对应原文 all of us participated in the food gathering task，这是所有人都参与的劳动，不是 blacksmith 的主要工作，故也排除。
答案	B

Question 15

题目定位词 / 关键词	like the most; varied activities; knowledge; exercise
录音原文定位	WOMAN: ... What would you say was the favourite part of your whole experience there, Jim? MAN: You know what, what I especially loved about the life there was everybody had many different things to do. We would never get bored. And we also gained some new knowledge from all sorts of activities. Another unexpected bonus was I even lost some weight at the end of the program. I guess it was due to all the physical work every day.
题目解释	题干：Jim 最喜欢这个村子的什么地方？ A：人们有各种不同的活动 B：人们分享他们的知识 C：人们得到很多锻炼 由 like the most 可定位至女士的提问 What would you say was the favourite part of your whole experience there（the favourite part 同义替换 like the most）。Jim 回答特别喜欢那里的生活，因为每个人都有很多不同的事情要做，由此可知答案为选项 A，其中 varied activities 对应 many different things to do。选项 B 对应原文 And we also gained some new knowledge from all sorts of activities，但这只是众多活动中的一方面，故排除选项 B。选项 C 原文未提及，虽然后文 Jim 提到减了点体重，但那是因为每天要做很多体力活，故也排除。
答案	A

Test 5 解析

Questions 16-20

题型：**流程图题**

Question 16

题目定位词 / 关键词	Mark; centre
录音原文定位	You decide the centre point and use the pegs to mark it out.
题目解释	根据题干可知，空格处应该填写某种工具的名称，与 centre 有关。根据 centre 定位到听力原文 decide the centre point and use the pegs to mark it out，由此可知答案为 G (pegs)。
答案	G

Question 17

题目定位词 / 关键词	Dig some holes; animal
录音原文定位	So, in order to do that, next you need to dig in your marks and make some room for the posts. You will use some special hand-made tools, which come from animal bones.
题目解释	根据题干可知，空格处应该填写名词，且与动物有关。根据题干的关键词可定位到听力原文 next you need to dig in...which come from animal bones，由此可知这些工具是用动物的骨头做的，答案为 D (bones)。
答案	D

Question 18

题目定位词 / 关键词	Drive the posts; holes
录音原文定位	After that, you can fix those wooden posts, usually made of hazel branches, into the holes.
题目解释	根据题干可知，空格处应该填写一个名词，是构成 posts 的材料。根据 posts 定位到听力原文 you can fix those wooden posts... 原文说这些 posts 通常是由 hazel branches 制成的，fix 对应题干中的 drive，into the holes 原词重现，由此可知答案为 F (hazel)。
答案	F

Question 19

题目定位词 / 关键词	roof; help
录音原文定位	With the walls of the roundhouse completed, you can climb up to the scaffold and start building the roof.
题目解释	根据题干可知，空格处应该填写一个名词，表示在某物的帮助下盖屋顶。根据 roof 定位到听力原文 you can climb up to the scaffold and start building the roof，由此可知答案为 E (scaffold)。
答案	E

Question 20

题目定位词 / 关键词	roof poles; make sure; length
录音原文定位	The first thing you need to do is to raise the roof poles and bind them together with rope using more hazel rods. But before that, you should check that the roof poles are of equal length.
题目解释	根据题干可知，空格处应该填写一个形容词，修饰 length。根据 length 可定位到听力原文 you should check that the roof poles are of equal length，check 对应题干中的 make sure，由此可知答案为 C (equal)。
答案	C

场景词汇

单词	音标	词性	释义	单词	音标	词性	释义
participate	/pɑːˈtɪsɪpeɪt/	v.	参加	occasion	/əˈkeɪʒn/	n.	场合；时刻，时候
exhausted	/ɪgˈzɔːstɪd/	adj.	筋疲力尽的；耗尽的	gathering	/ˈɡæðərɪŋ/	n.	搜集，采集
priority	/praɪˈɒrəti/	n.	优先事项，最重要的事	blacksmith	/ˈblæksmɪθ/	n.	铁匠
fulfilling	/fʊlˈfɪlɪŋ/	adj.	令人满足的，使人有成就感的	procedure	/prəˈsiːdʒə(r)/	n.	步骤，程序
location	/ləʊˈkeɪʃn/	n.	地点，位置				

拓展词汇 |

单词	音标	词性	释义	单词	音标	词性	释义
replicate	/ˈreplɪkeɪt/	v.	重复，复制	Iron Age		phr.	铁器时代
rise	/raɪz/	v.	起床	put somebody off		phr.	使某人失去兴趣
in no time		phr.	很快，立刻	bonus	/ˈbəʊnəs/	n.	意外收获，额外好处
prominent	/ˈprɒmɪnənt/	adj.	重要的，著名的	available	/əˈveɪləbl/	adj.	可用的，可获得的
peg	/peg/	n.	挂钩，挂钉	perimeter	/pəˈrɪmɪtə(r)/	n.	周长，外围
daub	/dɔːb/	n.	涂抹；涂料	pliable	/ˈplaɪəbl/	adj.	柔韧的，易曲折的
manure	/məˈnjʊə(r)/	n.	肥料	scaffold	/ˈskæfəʊld/	n.	脚手架
thatch	/θætʃ/	n.	茅草，杂草				

Part 3　*Questions 21-30*

场景介绍 |

主题场景	商业经营	考查题型	选择题（单项）+ 选择题（多项）
主旨大意	导师和两名学生讨论品牌重塑的定义、案例以及与项目管理的联系		

逐题精讲 |

Questions 21-26

　题型：选择题（单项）

Question 21

题目定位词 / 关键词	shortcoming; definition of branding; only focuses on sellers; too much information; too narrow
录音原文定位	**TUTOR:** Um, what do you think of this definition? **SUE:** Well...it only mentioned products and services, but I think branding should include a wider range of aspects, such as product quality, culture, customers as well as marketing strategies, and so on.
题目解释	题干：AMA 目前对品牌的定义最大的缺陷是什么？ A：它只专注于卖方 B：它包含了太多信息 C：它太狭隘了 当听到导师的提问 what do you think of this definition 时，预示答案即将出现。Sue 回答它只提到了产品和服务，还应该包括其他方面，这意味着 Sue 认为该定义是狭隘的，由此可知答案为选项 C。选项 A 与原文不符，原文说的是 only mentioned products and services，故排除。选项 B 与原文矛盾，Sue 认为该定义过于狭隘，故也排除。
答案	C

Question 22

题目定位词 / 关键词	cause; company's bankruptcy; changed its logo; not adapt to the current situation, not get enough funding support
录音原文定位	However, blinded by their temporary success, they thought they had no need to re-brand. So later on, when the commercial market changed rapidly, they fell behind in the competition.

	题干：两名学生都认可的导致公司破产的原因是什么？ A：公司改变了 logo B：公司没有适应当前的形势 C：公司没有得到足够的资金支持
题目解释	用 bankruptcy 去定位，Tom 提到 declared bankruptcy because of its failure in branding，紧接着导师提问是如何失败的，Sue 回答该公司被暂时的成功蒙蔽了双眼（blinded by their temporary success），认为没有必要重新打造品牌，后来当商业市场瞬息万变时，他们在竞争中落在了后面（fell behind in the competition），这意味着该公司没有适应当前形势，由此可知答案为选项 B。选项 A 不是失败的原因，事实上新 logo 还帮助公司获得了一大笔投资，得到了一时的繁荣（because this new logo helped them gain a vast amount of investment and they went through a period of great prosperity），故排除。选项 C 与原文 gain a vast amount of investment（得到了一笔巨大的投资）矛盾，故也排除。
答案	B

Question 23

题目定位词 / 关键词	want to learn; project management; in a team; transferability; constraints
录音原文定位	But what I am really concerned about is whether this practice can be applied to marketing.
	题干：Sue 想了解项目管理的什么方面？ A：它是如何在团队中运作的 B：它向其他方面的转移性 C：流程中的限制
题目解释	用 project management 去定位，Sue 说 Oh, and I also read some books about project management，接着介绍了 project management 的含义，通过 But 转折，提出自己真正关心的是它是否能应用到市场营销上（But what I am really concerned about is whether this practice can be applied to marketing），句中 this practice 指代上文的 project management，由此可知答案为选项 B，其中 transferability（可转移性，通用性）对应原文中的 can be applied to，other aspects 对应原文中的 marketing。选项 A 和 C 均在原文中有所涉及（It's mainly about how to lead a team to achieve their goals within certain limitations, like time, budget, and scope），但不是 Sue 真正想知道的，故均排除。
答案	B

Question 24

题目定位词 / 关键词	recommend; book; re-branding; clear
录音原文定位	**TOM:** Well, this book is continually being updated with lots of real-life examples. <u>And the structure is pretty well-organized.</u> I think, for those who are just getting started in the industry, it's easy to digest.
题目解释	题干：Tom 推荐给 Sue 此书的原因是什么？ A：这本书适合有一定基础的人 B：内容恰好是关于品牌重塑的 C：这本书非常清晰 根据题干中的关键词可定位至 Tom 的话，Tom 提到 I also read a book called... 紧接着 Sue 问这本书有何特别之处，预示答案即将出现。Tom 回答这本书的结构很 well-organized（有条理的），由此可知答案为选项 C。选项 A 与原文意思相反，原文说的是 for those who are just getting started in the industry，即这本书适合新手，而不是有一定基础的人，故排除。选项 B precisely on re-branding 在原文中未提及，故也排除。
答案	C

Question 25

题目定位词 / 关键词	Tom like about; e-mail; historical use; practical information; research model
录音原文定位	**TOM:** At the beginning, it introduces the history of the company, <u>and then it provides many details about how the people in the focus group were gathered, which gave me a lot of inspiration.</u> **SUE:** Right. Also, I think its layout can be regarded as a good sample which we can definitely learn from.
题目解释	题干：Tom 对 Sue 邮件中发给他的文章的看法是什么？ A：它提供了关于焦点小组的历史用途的消息 B：它为组建焦点小组提供了实用的信息 C：它可以被用作一个研究模型 根据 e-mail 可定位至 Sue 的话，Sue 提到 have you read the e-mail that... 随后 Tom 提到给他印象最深的是文章里提到的 focus group（焦点小组），Tom 说这篇文章提供了许多关于焦点小组中的人是如何聚集在一起的细节，这给了他很多灵感，由此可知答案为选项 B，forming 对应原文中的 gathered。选项 A 为张冠李戴，原文是 the history of the company，故排除。选项 C 为下文 Sue 的观点（its layout can be regarded as a good sample），而非 Tom 的看法，故也排除。
答案	B

Question 26

题目定位词 / 关键词	small companies; easier; enough academic papers; first-hand experience
录音原文定位	**TUTOR:** Great. What kind of companies are you going to study? **SUE:** We both have experience with large companies. But we didn't find enough papers about big companies to support our study. And you know, Lichfield is just a small town, and local companies are all pretty small. We believe that it's important to be able to gather data first-hand, so we decided to focus on smaller companies.
题目解释	题干：两位同学为什么专注于研究小公司？ A：更容易开展当地研究 B：他们可以找到足够的关于小公司的学术论文 C：他们有在小公司工作的一手经验 当听到导师提问 What kind of companies are you going to study 时，预示答案即将出现，随后 Sue 回答说 Lichfield 是一个小镇，当地的公司都很小，能够收集第一手数据很重要，因此他们决定重点关注较小的公司。由此可知，专注于小公司的原因是方便他们收集数据、做研究，故答案为选项 A。选项 B 和 C 为张冠李戴。原文说的是 didn't find enough papers about big companies，这并不能说明他们可以找到足够的关于小公司的学术论文，故排除选项 B。选项 C 与原文不符，原文说他们均有大公司的经验，而非小公司的，故排除选项 C。
答案	A

Questions 27-30

题型：选择题（多项）

Questions 27-28

题目定位词 / 关键词	reasons, failure, re-branding, ice cream company, prices, a new ice cream formula, not receive enough funding, not use enough colors, adapted to a modern logo
录音原文定位	**SUE:** ...What I have studied is an ice cream company named Pure Scoop. They spent a large amount of money on the reconstruction of their logo. They have even recruited an Italian designer to change the colour schemes to follow the newest trends. However, this logo does not match the old-fashioned style the company represents, which makes it lose its unique appeal. **TUTOR:** That might be one reason for its failure. What else? **SUE:** The money spent on the logo also caused the costs to go up 2% and a pro-rata increase in ice cream prices. According to customers, the increased prices are acceptable, but what they cannot accept is the change in the recipes. Most of their customers have not gotten used to the new flavour.

题目解释	题干：冰淇淋公司品牌重塑失败的两个原因是什么？ A：它的价格急剧上涨 B：它换了一种新的冰淇淋配方 C：它的新 logo 没有得到足够的资金支持 D：它的新 logo 没有使用足够多的颜色 E：它采用了现代风格的 logo 由 ice cream company 可定位至 Sue 的话，Sue 提到 What I have studied is an ice cream company... 然后提及这个公司重塑品牌的事情，随后开始分析该公司品牌为什么重塑失败。转折词 However 后为失败的第一个原因，即新标志与公司所代表的老式风格不匹配（does not match the old-fashioned style the company represents），由此可知风格偏现代，所以选项 E 为正确选项。 紧接着导师询问其他原因，Sue 继续分析，答案出现在转折词 but 后，顾客不能接受食谱的改变（what they cannot accept is the change in the recipes），由此可知选项 B 为正确选项，formula 对应原文中的 recipes。 选项 A 不是失败的原因，原文说顾客认为提升后的价格是可以接受的（the increased prices are acceptable），故排除。 选项 C 与原文表述相矛盾，原文说他们在重塑 logo 上投入了大量的钱（They spent a large amount of money on the reconstruction of their logo），故排除。 选项 D 原文未提及，故排除。
答案	B E

Questions 29-30

题目定位词 / 关键词	factors; car-washing company; failed to monitor; changed its price structure; changed to an unpopular site; underestimated competitors; refocused its marketing strategy to luxury
录音原文定位	More specifically, when choosing a new site, they picked a place with few pedestrians and inconvenient transportation, leading to the shrinkage of their market share.Next, to differentiate itself from their competitors, the company began to target the luxury market. However, the economic situation here does not provide enough high-end customers for them to make ends meet.

题目解释	题干：洗车公司失败的两个因素是什么？ A：它没能监测品牌重塑活动 B：它改变了自己的价格结构 C：它换到了一个不受欢迎的场所 D：它低估了自己的竞争者 E：它重新将自己的营销策略定位于高端市场 根据 car-washing company 可定位至 Tom 的回答 I studied a car wash company... 后文均为针对该洗车公司品牌重塑的分析，当听到 the results were disappointing 时预示答案即将出现。第一个失败的原因为在选择新址时，他们选择了行人少、交通不便的地方，导致市场份额缩水，由此可知选项 C 为正确选项。 紧接着 Next 之后为第二个原因，即该公司开始瞄准奢侈品市场。然而，经济形势并没有为他们提供足够的高端客户，由此可知选项 E 为正确选项。 选项 A 和 B 与原文 They used brand-monitoring software to measure current brand perception and adjusted their price system. These measures helped them increase their brand's popularity for a while 矛盾，该公司使用品牌监测软件并调整了他们的价格体系，这些措施帮助他们在一段时间内提高了自己品牌的知名度。 选项 D 与原文表述相矛盾，因为他们曾试图向竞争对手学习（they also tried to learn from their competitors）。 综上，排除选项 A、B、D。
答案	C E

场景词汇

单词	音标	词性	释义	单词	音标	词性	释义
re-branding	/ˌriːˈbrændɪŋ/	n.	品牌重塑	identify	/aɪˈdentɪfaɪ/	v.	认出，识别
strategy	/ˈstrætədʒi/	n.	策略	enterprise	/ˈentəpraɪz/	n.	企业
bankruptcy	/ˈbæŋkrʌptsi/	n.	破产，倒闭	competition	/ˌkɒmpəˈtɪʃn/	n.	竞争
project management		phr.	项目管理	budget	/ˈbʌdʒɪt/	n.	预算
apply to		phr.	适用于，应用于	well-organized	/welˈɔːɡənaɪzd/	adj.	有序的；有条理的
first-hand	/ˌfɜːst ˈhænd/	adv.	直接地；第一手的				

拓展词汇 |

单词	音标	词性	释义	单词	音标	词性	释义
distinct	/dɪˈstɪŋkt/	adj.	不同的，有区别的	declare	/dɪˈkleə(r)/	v.	宣布
renowned	/rɪˈnaʊnd/	adj.	有名望的，著名的	redo	/ˌriːˈduː/	v.	重做
prosperity	/prɒˈsperəti/	n.	繁荣，成功	temporary	/ˈtemprəri/	adj.	暂时的
digest	/daɪˈdʒest/	v.	理解，领悟；消化	semi-structured	/ˈsemi ˈstrʌktʃəd/	adj.	半结构化的
conducive	/kənˈdjuːsɪv/	adj.	有助的，有益的	inspiration	/ˌɪnspəˈreɪʃn/	n.	灵感，启发

Part 4　*Questions 31-40*

场景介绍 ┃

主题场景	动植物		考查题型	笔记填空题
主旨大意	讲座讲述了非洲企鹅的栖息环境、生活习惯、生理特征以及生存状况			

逐题精讲 ┃

　　题型：**笔记填空题**

Question 31

题目定位词 / 关键词	Adaptation to climate; keep; bodies; constant
录音原文定位	In common with all penguins, they have to adapt to weather conditions so as to maintain a constant body temperature.
题目解释	根据题干可知，空格处应该填入一个名词，与非洲企鹅的身体有关。根据关键词可定位至 they have to adapt to weather conditions so as to maintain a constant body temperature，意思是它们必须适应天气条件以保持恒定的体温。weather conditions 对应题干中的 climate，maintain 对应题干中的 keep，由此可知答案为 temperature。
答案	temperature

Question 32

题目定位词 / 关键词	Restrict; dawn and dusk
录音原文定位	One of the ways they do this is by confining their movement into early evening and early morning.
题目解释	根据题干可知，空格处应该填入一个名词，作为 restrict 的宾语。根据关键词可定位至 by confining their movement into early evening and early morning，意思是将活动限制在清晨和傍晚。confining 对应题干中的 restrict，early evening and early morning 对应题干中的 dawn and dusk，由此可知答案为 movement。
答案	movement

Question 33

题目定位词 / 关键词	nests; under tree
录音原文定位	Also in order to protect themselves from the intense heat of the daytime sun, they establish their homes by making hollows or nests beneath the roots of trees.
题目解释	根据题干可知，空格处应该填写一个名词，与 nests 的位置有关，由此可定位至 they establish their homes by making hollows or nests beneath the roots of trees，意思是它们通过在树根下挖洞或筑巢来建立家园。establish 对应题干中的 set up，beneath（在……下方）对应题干中的 under，由此可知答案为 roots。
答案	roots

Question 34

题目定位词 / 关键词	Unable to fly; because of; heavy
录音原文定位	This is due to them having solid and very dense bones.
题目解释	根据题干可知，空格处应该填写一个名词，表示不能飞的原因，由此可定位到 can swim but can't fly，随后解释了不能飞的原因，即 This is due to them having solid and very dense bones（因为它们有坚固而致密的骨骼）。due to 对应题干中的 because of，solid and dense 对应题干中的 heavy，由此可知答案为 bones。
答案	bones

Question 35

题目定位词 / 关键词	Annual moult; lose; three weeks
录音原文定位	The entire period of shedding feathers takes about 20 days to complete.
题目解释	根据题干可知，空格处应该填写一个名词，作为 lose 的宾语。根据关键词可定位至 An interesting factor related to their eating patterns is the annual moult（脱羽），随后提到 The entire period of shedding feathers takes about 20 days to complete，意思是整个脱羽期大约需要 20 天才能完成。shedding（脱落）对应题干中的 lose，about 20 days 对应题干中的 three weeks，由此可知答案为 feathers。
答案	feathers

Question 36

题目定位词 / 关键词	Threats to survival; industrial fishing; and
录音原文定位	However, this has changed with current factors being primarily overfishing by commercial boat and pollution.
题目解释	根据题干可知，空格处应该填写一个名词，与 industrial fishing 并列，作为企鹅生存的威胁，由此可定位至 let's move on to consider some of the major threats to their survival，随后提到非洲企鹅近年数量减少的原因，转折词 However 后提到 current factors being primarily overfishing by commercial boat and pollution，意思是目前的因素主要是商业渔船的过度捕捞和污染，commercial 对应题干中的 industrial，由此可知答案为 pollution。
答案	pollution

Question 37

题目定位词 / 关键词	Competition; and; food; seals
录音原文定位	Aside from these man-made causes, there is also fierce competition with seals for space in which to live, and also for food.
题目解释	根据题干可知，空格处应该填入一个名词，这个名词与 food 并列，也是与海豹竞争的一样东西，由此可定位至 fierce competition with seals for space in which to live, and also for food，意思是除了与海豹竞争食物，还会竞争生存空间，由此可知答案为 space。
答案	space

Question 38

题目定位词 / 关键词	predators; sea lions
录音原文定位	These penguins also face attacks from sharks, which pose a large problem.
题目解释	根据题干可知，空格处应该填入一个名词，和 sea lions 并列，是非洲企鹅生存的天敌之一，由此可定位至 These penguins also face attacks from sharks，意思是这些企鹅还面临着鲨鱼的攻击。sea lions 在下一句中也被提到了，说另一个天敌是海狮（Another such predaceous sea mammal for them is the sea lion）。predaceous 对应题干中的 predators，由此可知答案为 sharks。
答案	sharks

Question 39

题目定位词 / 关键词	seagulls; eat the penguins'
录音原文定位	Threats can also come from the air, with gulls preying on the penguin chicks.
题目解释	本题仍停留在捕食企鹅的动物上。根据题干可知，空格处应该填入一个名词，范围缩小到捕食企鹅的某样东西。根据顺序可定位至 gulls preying on the penguin chicks，也就是说海鸥会捕食企鹅的幼崽。gulls 对应题干中的 seagulls，preying on 对应题干中的 eat，由此可知答案为 chicks。
答案	chicks

Question 40

题目定位词 / 关键词	preservation; Keep; in genes
录音原文定位	The aim is to be able to maintain a healthy diversity genetically within the population across the continent over a very long period of time.
题目解释	根据题干可知，空格处应该填入一个名词，与 preservation 的方法有关，具体内容又与 genes 有关。根据关键词可定位至 preservation is hugely important，随后提到 to maintain a healthy diversity genetically，意思是保持健康的遗传多样性，maintain 对应题干中的 keep，genetically 对应题干中的 in genes，由此可知答案为 diversity。
答案	diversity

场景词汇

单词	音标	词性	释义	单词	音标	词性	释义
marine	/məˈriːn/	adj.	海洋的	mammal	/ˈmæml/	n.	哺乳动物
confine	/kənˈfaɪn/	v.	限制	constant	/ˈkɒnstənt/	adj.	恒定的
physiological	/ˌfɪziəˈlɒdʒɪkl /	adj.	生理（学）的	moult	/məʊlt/	v.	（动物）脱毛，换羽
shed	/ʃed/	v.	（动物）蜕（皮），脱（毛）	feather	/ˈfeðə(r)/	n..	羽毛
endangered	/ɪnˈdeɪndʒəd/	adj.	（动植物）濒危的	species	/ˈspiːʃiːz/	n.	（动植物的）种，物种；种类
exploitation	/ˌeksplɔɪˈteɪʃn/	n.	利用	predaceous	/prɪˈdeɪʃəs/	adj.	食肉的；捕食生物的
prey on		phr.	捕食	preservation	/ˌprezəˈveɪʃn/	n.	保护，维护
breed	/briːd/	v.	交配繁殖；培育	diversity	/daɪˈvɜːsəti/	n.	多样性
adaptation	/ˌædæpˈteɪʃn/	n.	适应	predator	/ˈpredətə(r)/	n.	捕食性动物；掠夺者

拓展词汇 |

单词	音标	词性	释义	单词	音标	词性	释义
Antarctic	/æn'tɑːktɪk/	n.	南极洲	hemisphere	/'hemɪsfɪə(r)/	n.	（地球的）半球
offshore	/ˌɒf'ʃɔː(r)/	adj.	近海的，离岸的	hollow	/'hɒləʊ/	n./adj.	洞，坑 / 空的
pant	/pænt/	v.	气喘，喘息	skeletal	/'skelətl/	adj.	骨骼的
vary	/'veəri/	v.	（使）不同;（根据情况而）变化	considerably	/kən'sɪdərəbli/	adv.	非常，相当多地
occurrence	/ə'kʌrəns/	n.	发生，出现	astonishing	/ə'stɒnɪʃɪŋ/	adj.	惊人的，令人惊讶的

Test 5 解析

Test 6 解析

Part 1　*Questions 1-10*

场景介绍

主题场景	日常咨询	考查题型	笔记填空题
主旨大意	一位女士打电话咨询体育营的活动		

逐题精讲

题型：**笔记填空题**

Question 1

题目定位词 / 关键词	baseball; tennis and
录音原文定位	**WOMAN:** Right. What classes do you have then? **MAN:** Well, we offer some classes for ball games, such as baseball classes and tennis classes. Basketball classes are likely to be introduced, but we need to double check the schedule with the coach. Also, you can join swimming classes if your kid is interested in water sports.
题目解释	根据题干可知，空格处应该填写与 baseball 和 tennis 并列且表示某种运动的名词。女士问有什么课程，男士首先提到了 baseball 和 tennis，随后提到 basketball，但是又补充说需要与教练确认一下，因此答案不是 basketball。男士继续介绍说可以加入 swimming classes，由此可知答案为 swimming。
答案	swimming

Question 2

题目定位词 / 关键词	venue; Street
录音原文定位	**MAN:** The classes start on the 1st of June and goes on till the 25th, and all the classes will be held at High Street.
题目解释	根据题干中的 venue 可知，空格处应该填写体育营开办的地点，答案应为一个街道名称。Street 的 S 大写，由此可以判断所填单词应该跟 Street 合在一起表示一个地址，Street 不会被替换，因此可以直接用 Street 定位。工作人员介绍了体育营课程的时间，紧接着说所有的课程都在 High Street 上课，由此可知答案为 High。
答案	High

Question 3

题目定位词 / 关键词	improve children's skills and
录音原文定位	**WOMAN:** ...Do you have soccer classes? He is a big fan of soccer and dreams to be a football player in the future. **MAN:** Sure. We have exceptional soccer pitches available for our membership. <u>Our sport-specific staff will ensure that your young athlete will gain some new skills and improve his physical fitness through the soccer class.</u>
题目解释	根据题干可知，空格处填写的单词应与 skills 并列，两者属于 Soccer class 可以帮助孩子们提升的方面。女士问有没有 soccer classes，工作人员在介绍 soccer classes 时提到会获得一些新的技能，并且提高身体素质，其中 young athlete 对应题干中的 children，gain some new skills 对应题干中的 improve the children's skills，因此 physical fitness 为答案。但本题要求答案只填写一个单词，且此空格处只能填写名词，所以正确答案为 fitness。
答案	fitness

Question 4

题目定位词 / 关键词	staff; provide a
录音原文定位	**WOMAN:** Sounds great. Do we need to bring anything? A helmet, knee pads, soccer ball... **MAN:** No. <u>No need to bring any equipment, and the ball will be provided by us.</u>
题目解释	根据题干可知，空格处应该填写一个单数可数名词，是营地员工提供的某种物品。当女士提问 Do we need to bring anything 时预示答案即将出现，工作人员回答说不用带任何设备，我们会提供球，所以工作人员会提供的东西是 ball。
答案	ball

Question 5

题目定位词 / 关键词	Children; wear a
录音原文定位	**MAN:** ...But it will be really hot in June, so I guess your son could wear a hat to protect himself from the searing sun.
题目解释	本题仍在介绍 Soccer class，根据题干可知，空格处应该填写一个单数可数名词，是工作人员建议孩子穿戴的某种物品。工作人员说 your son could wear a hat to protect，son 对应题干中的 children，所以答案为 hat。
答案	hat

Question 6

题目定位词 / 关键词	Senior Group Activities; A talk
录音原文定位	**MAN:** Then the senior group will be a perfect fit for him. It's for older kids and also for beginner to intermediate-level players. **WOMAN:** Are there any other activities in this group? **MAN:** We've planned a talk, and the topic is about how to balance your diet, which I believe is worth listening to.
题目解释	根据题干可知，空格处应该填写一个名词，是 Senior group activities 中谈论的主题。根据 senior group 首先可定位至 Then the senior group will be a perfect fit，随后女士提问 Are there any other activities in this group? 这预示着答案即将出现。紧接着工作人员回答已经计划了一场 talk，话题是 how to balance your diet，也就是说 talk 的主题是怎样平衡你的膳食，由此可知答案为 diet。
答案	diet

Question 7

题目定位词 / 关键词	a talent show and a
录音原文定位	**MAN:** After the class, there are several activities for fun as well. For example, the talent show, which allows their personality to shine. And we've noticed that many kids are passionate about competition, so we've decided to organize one to boost their enthusiasm for sports and teach them how to collaborate with teammates.
题目解释	根据题干可知，空格处应该填写一个单数名词，且是与 talent show 并列的某种活动。当工作人员说 For example, the talent show 时预示答案即将出现，随后听到并列连词 And 及后面的内容 we've noticed that many kids are passionate about competition, so we've decided to organize one to...(我们注意到很多孩子喜欢比赛，所以我们觉得组织一场比赛……)，整个句子中只有 competition 符合要求，由此可知答案为 competition。
答案	competition

Question 8

题目定位词 / 关键词	competition; begins at; on June 15th
录音原文定位	**WOMAN:** ...When should we arrive there? **MAN:** The time for the talent show has not been decided yet, but the competition will be held on June 15th, starting at 4:30 p.m..
题目解释	根据题干可知，空格处应该填写 competition 开始的时间。空格后面给出了 June 15th 这样的日期，那么 at 之后就应该填写具体的时间。当女士提问 When should we arrive there 时预示答案即将出现，随后工作人员回答比赛将在 June 15th, 4:30 p.m. 开始，由此可知答案为 4:30 p.m.。
答案	4:30 p.m.

Question 9

题目定位词 / 关键词	staff; Emma
录音原文定位	**MAN:** ...When you get there, you should contact Emma Costa. **WOMAN:** Sorry, Emma... **MAN:** Costa. C-O-S-T-A.
题目解释	根据题干可知，空格处应填写工作人员的名字。工作人员提到 When you get there, you should contact Emma Costa，当女士表示迟疑后，工作人员告知了其名字的拼写 C-O-S-T-A，由此可知答案为 Costa。
答案	Costa

Question 10

题目定位词 / 关键词	Telephone number
录音原文定位	**MAN:** ... Also, you can call her on her phone. Her number is zero four one nine, five four three, double two eight.
题目解释	根据题干可知，空格处应填写一串电话号码。当工作人员提到 Also, you can call her on her phone 时预示答案即将出现，随后马上提到了一串数字，由此可知答案为 0419543228。
答案	0419543228

场景词汇

单词	音标	词性	释义	单词	音标	词性	释义
suitable	/ˈsuːtəbl/	adj.	适宜的，合适的	schedule	/ˈʃedjuːl/	n.	计划（表）；课程表
coach	/kəʊtʃ/	n.	教练	venue	/ˈvenjuː/	n.	（活动的）场所
pitch	/pɪtʃ/	n.	体育场地，球场	membership	/ˈmembəʃɪp/	n.	会员身份，会籍
physical fitness		phr.	身体健康	professional	/prəˈfeʃənl/	adj.	职业的，专业的
senior	/ˈsiːniə(r)/	adj.	年龄大些的，较高级的	intermediate	/ˌɪntəˈmiːdiət/	adj.	中间的；中等程度的，中级的
registration	/ˌredʒɪˈstreɪʃn/	n.	登记，注册				

拓展词汇 |

单词	音标	词性	释义	单词	音标	词性	释义
Melbourne	/ˈmelbən/	n.	墨尔本	locate	/ləʊˈkeɪt/	v.	位于……
exceptional	/ɪkˈsepʃənl/	adj.	卓越的，杰出的	searing	/ˈsɪərɪŋ/	adj.	灼热的
currently	/ˈkʌrəntli/	adv.	现时，当前	personality	/ˌpɜːsəˈnæləti/	n.	个性，性格
passionate	/ˈpæʃənət/	adj.	热诚的，狂热的	enthusiasm	/ɪnˈθjuːziæzəm/	n.	热情，热忱
collaborate	/kəˈlæbəreɪt/	v.	合作，协作	strain	/streɪn/	v.	损伤，扭伤；压力
originally	/əˈrɪdʒənəli/	adv.	起初，原来				

Test 6 解析

Part 2　　*Questions 11-20*

场景介绍 |

主题场景	旅游度假	考查题型	选择题（单项）+ 选择题（多项）
主旨大意	一位男士向游客介绍即将到来的昆士兰的节日活动		

逐题精讲 |

Questions 11-16

　　题型：选择题（单项）

Question 11

题目定位词 / 关键词	Why; recommend; Tuesday; entrance is free; fewer people; different educational classes
录音原文定位	As is shown on our website, you will not be charged for admission on weekends. But as you can imagine, it will be very crowded, so I strongly recommend you to visit here on Tuesday, unless you want to see a sea of people.
题目解释	题干：为什么 James 推荐周二去那里？ A：因为门票免费 B：人比较少 C：提供不一样的教育课程 题干问为什么推荐周二去那里，由此可知应该去找表达因果逻辑的句子。录音中男士先提到周末是不收费的，但是紧接着又说非常挤，所以推荐周二去，故推荐周二去的原因是周二人较少，答案为选项 B。门票在周末是免费的，不是周二免费，所以排除选项 A。选项 C 在所有日期都提供，不是只有周二才提供（No matter what day of the week it is, you can join some classes together with your kids, learning about geography, history, art and so on），故排除选项 C。
答案	B

Question 12

题目定位词 / 关键词	educational talk; held; weekends; evening; afternoon
录音原文定位	Originally, it was only held on weekends, but later it became so popular that we changed its schedule, so now you can take part in the talk on any given afternoon.

题目解释	题干：教育讲座在什么时候举行？ A：周末 B：每个晚上 C：每个下午 根据 educational talk 可定位至 Also, we will organize an educational talk... 随后男士说起初只在周末举办，但后来变得很受欢迎，就改变了时间表，可以在任何一个下午参加讲座 (so now you can take part in the talk on any given afternoon)，由此可知答案为选项 C。选项 A 是原来的时间安排，不符合现有的情况，故排除。选项 B 与原文矛盾，故也排除。
答案	C

Question 13

题目定位词 / 关键词	buy tickets; in the library; cheaper; receive a lovely book; convenient
录音原文定位	Tickets there are cheaper than if you buy them in the city because you'll get an 80% discount.
题目解释	题干：人们为什么在图书馆买票？ A：更便宜 B：会提前得到一本可爱的书 C：比在城市买票方便 根据 buy tickets 首先可定位至 You will get a pamphlet showing you the sites of where you can buy tickets to the show，意味着接下来要介绍买票的地点。随后去找关键词 library，当听到 so it will take you almost the same amount of time to get to the library in the suburbs（去市区和去郊区的图书馆花费的时间一样多）时，答案还未出现，紧接着男士说 Tickets there are cheaper than if you buy them in the city（在那里买票比市区便宜），there 指代 library，由此可知答案为选项 A。 选项 B a lovely book 指原文中的 pamphlet（小册子），但小册子只是告诉你去哪里买票，不符合题目要求。 选项 C 与原文不符，因为原文提到去城市的购买点和去郊区图书馆花费的时间基本相同。
答案	A

Question 14

题目定位词 / 关键词	interest history lovers; most; garden; architecture; location
录音原文定位	But it was not until 1606 that the Dutch explorer Willem Jansz first landed on the Cape York Peninsula, and the castle was built right on his landing site.

题目解释	题干：历史爱好者最感兴趣的可能是什么？ A：花园 B：建筑设计 C：位置 根据 history lovers 可定位至 It's a perfect place for those who love history because the castle is of great historical importance，即城堡具有重要的历史意义。紧接着后文解释了历史意义是城堡建在著名探险家的登陆点上（the castle was built right on his landing site），因此历史爱好者感兴趣的是城堡的地点，由此可知答案为选项 C。 选项 A 和 B 均在原文有所提及（you will see a fascinating garden; it typifies some of the early Queensland architectural style），但与 history lovers 无关，故均排除。
答案	C

Question 15

题目定位词 / 关键词	special; Cuisine Festival; a wider range of activities; well-known musician; luxury hotels and international chefs
录音原文定位	During the event, a popular singer who has won many national awards will meet us and share his new songs.
题目解释	题干：今年的美食节有什么特别之处？ A：比往年的活动范围更广 B：一个知名的音乐家将参加 C：有豪华饭店和国际厨师 根据 Cuisine Festival 首先可定位至 Next is one of our most popular events—the Food Festival，随后去找本次美食节的特别之处，即 a popular singer who has won many national awards will meet us and share his new songs，由此可知答案为选项 B。 选项 A 为无关比较，原文并未提及现在的活动比以前多，原文只说地点比之前更大（the camping tent in that area is much bigger than last year's），故排除。 选项 C 原文未提及，原文只提到 local chefs，故也排除。
答案	B

Question 16

题目定位词 / 关键词	exhibition; visitors; allowed; watch a display; dress up old uniform costumes; have a dinner
录音原文定位	Although you won't be able to see how the steam engines operate, you can enjoy meals with your family in the railway carriage after 6:00 p.m.

题目解释	题干：在展览上游客可以做什么？ A：观看一场蒸汽机如何工作的表演 B：穿上以前的服装 C：在火车厢里吃晚饭 根据题干可定位至 In the exhibition, you can learn how to... 首先听到能做的事情是 identify steam locomotives（识别蒸汽机车），接着说虽然不能看到蒸汽机是如何工作的（排除选项 A），但是可以在下午 6 点后跟家人一起在火车厢共进晚餐，由此可知答案为选项 C，cabinet 对应原文中的 carriage。 选项 B 原文虽有提及，但不是游客 dress up，而是展览的一部分（Near the carriage will be an exhibition of the old uniforms），故排除。
答案	C

Questions 17-20

题型：选择题（多项）

Questions 17-18

题目定位词 / 关键词	included; family ticket; toy; book; free meal; guided tour; flag
录音原文定位	With the ticket stub, the staff will give you a colourful flag to wave. What your kids are allowed to take is the book on the bookshelf, which introduces the development of trams and trolleybuses.
题目解释	题干：家庭票包含什么？ A：一个玩具 B：一本给孩子的书 C：火车上的一次免费餐 D：导游带领参观布里斯班电车博物馆 E：一面旗帜 根据 family ticket 首先可定位至 If you plan to visit there with your family, the family ticket is good value for money，随后开始介绍 family ticket 所包含和不包含的内容。 第一处信息点为 the staff will give you a colourful flag to wave，因此选项 E 为正确答案之一。第二处信息点提到 What your kids are allowed to take is the book on the bookshelf，因此选项 B 也是正确的。 选项 A 在原文中虽有所提及，但仅仅是装饰作用（Some dolls, model cars and toy robots will be placed on the table in the museum just for decoration），故排除。 选项 C 和 D 均需花额外的钱才能获得（with another 5 pounds, you can get a meal voucher and enjoy your meal in a train cabin with your family ; you can hire our trained guide to give you more information, and that will cost you 6 pounds per hour），故也排除。
答案	B E

Test 6 解析

Questions 19-20

题目定位词/关键词	vote; the most popular event; any age; through e-mail; local people; several times; end at midnight on Saturday
录音原文定位	All the migrants and travellers, not just the people living there, have the right to vote, regardless of your age. Everyone has one vote per day, but after midnight, you will get a chance to vote again.
题目解释	题干：关于最受欢迎的活动的投票，哪两个说法是正确的？ A：任何年龄都可以参加投票 B：人们可以通过电子邮件投票 C：只有当地人能投票 D：人们可以多次投票 E：投票将在星期六的午夜结束 根据关键词可定位至 Every year, we will vote for the most popular annual event... 随后提到 All the migrants and travellers... have the right to vote, regardless of your age, 即移民、游客都可以参加投票，而且不管年龄大小都可以参加，所以选项 A 正确，选项 C 错误。 后文又提到 Everyone has one vote per day, but after midnight, you will get a chance to vote again, 即每天只能投一票，第二天可以再次投票，因此选项 D 也正确。 选项 B 与原文表述不符，原文说的是通过手机短信投票（Hit your new message button）。 选项 E 与原文表述不符，星期六午夜结束的是 activities, 而 voting 会在活动后的三天结束（All the activities will end on Saturday night and the voting phone lines will close at midnight three days after that）。
答案	A D

场景词汇 |

单词	音标	词性	释义	单词	音标	词性	释义
upcoming	/ˈʌpkʌmɪŋ/	adj.	即将来临的	charge	/tʃɑːdʒ/	v.	要价，收费
admission	/ədˈmɪʃn/	n.	进入权；入场费	pamphlet	/ˈpæmflət/	n.	小册子，活页
discount	/ˈdɪskaʊnt/	n.	折扣	hot spot		phr.	热门地区
specialty	/ˈspeʃəlti/	n.	特色食品，特产	character	/ˈkærəktə(r)/	n.	人物，角色
decoration	/ˌdekəˈreɪʃn/	n.	装饰	fringe benefit		phr.	附加福利
voucher	/ˈvaʊtʃə(r)/	n.	代金券，票券				

拓展词汇 |

单词	音标	词性	释义	单词	音标	词性	释义
interaction	/ˌɪntərˈækʃən/	n.	互动，交流	severe	/sɪˈvɪə(r)/	adj.	严重的，恶劣的
typify	/ˈtɪpɪfaɪ/	v.	作为……的典型；具有……的特点	architecture	/ˈɑːkɪtektʃə(r)/	n.	建筑设计；建筑学
locomotive	/ˌləʊkəˈməʊtɪv/	n.	机车，火车头	steam engine		phr.	蒸汽机
carriage	/ˈkærɪdʒ/	n.	（火车）车厢	ticket stub		phr.	票根
migrant	/ˈmaɪɡrənt/	n.	移民	regardless of		phr.	不顾，不管

Part 3　　*Questions 21-30*

场景介绍 |

主题场景	课程作业	考查题型	选择题（单项）+ 配对题
主旨大意	两名学生讨论最近发现的一处墓地的考古研究，并计划就此写一篇文章		

逐题精讲 |

Questions 21-25

　　题型：**选择题（单项）**

Question 21

题目定位词 / 关键词	impressed; female student; silver bowls; volunteers' behaviour; response archaeologists; students' work
录音原文定位	**WOMAN:** ... And what struck me most was that even though some archaeologists were not at the scene, they were as excited as if they had found the burial themselves.
题目解释	题干：女同学对银碗的发现印象最深的是什么？ A：志愿者们的行为 B：其他考古学家的反应 C：学生们的工作 根据题干信息可定位至女同学的话 And what struck me most was... 原文说即使一些考古学家不在现场，他们也像是自己发现了墓穴一样兴奋。因此，让女同学印象最深刻的是考古学家对发现银碗的反应，由此可知答案为选项 B。 选项 A 是下文男同学提到的内容（thanks to the volunteers, they did a very good job of preserving the archaeological site），而题目问的是女同学，故排除。 选项 C 在原文未提及，故也排除。
答案	B

Question 22

题目定位词 / 关键词	both agree; belonged to the church; buried with a person; sent to the museum
录音原文定位	**WOMAN:** Do you have any idea where the silver bowl come from? Is it possible that it belonged to the church? **MAN:** No, I don't think so. At that time, the church placed a unique pattern on everything it owned. But you can't find the special pattern on this bowl. **WOMAN:** You're right. I think it's more likely to be a rich man's burial object. **MAN:** Very likely, because a skeleton of a man was discovered accompanying it.

题目解释	题干：他们都同意银碗 ____。 A：属于教堂 B：是跟人一起埋下去的 C：应该被送去博物馆 通过三个选项可预判本题考查的是两人关于 silver bowl 归属的态度，由此可定位到女同学的提问 Do you have any idea where the silver bowl come from? 随后两人首先否定了 belonged to the church，故排除选项 A。之后女同学说银碗更有可能是富人的墓葬物品（a rich man's burial object），男同学表示赞同（Very likely），由此可知答案为选项 B。 选项 C 虽在原文中有所提及，但不是表达是否应该（should）送去博物馆，而是这些考古发现已经被送去博物馆了（All of these discoveries have been sent to the local museum），故排除选项 C。
答案	B

Question 23

题目定位词 / 关键词	plan; in the afternoon; divide up the assignment; collect visual resources; write up the essay
录音原文定位	**WOMAN:** Great. So going back to our essay, I think we already have enough material for it. Shall we try to finish it this afternoon? **MAN:** Well, I have to say that you're being too ambitious. We are far from writing up the essay because there are tons of other things to do, like, first, finding some images and videos related to the excavation and sorting them out, and then preparing the slides, deciding the research method... **WOMAN:** Oh, you're right. How about completing the first step this afternoon? **MAN:** That sounds reasonable.
题目解释	题干：他们计划下午做什么？ A：分配任务 B：收集视觉资料 C：写论文 根据题干可定位到女同学的提问 Shall we try to finish it this afternoon? 女同学提出要完成论文，但是男同学首先表示下午完成论文不现实（too ambitious），需要先做很多准备，如找到与挖掘相关的图片和视频，并进行整理，随后女同学表示同意，并建议下午先完成第一个。由男同学的回答 reasonable 可知答案为选项 B，visual resources 对应原文中的 images and videos。 选项 A 在原文中未提及，故排除。选项 C 与原文表述矛盾，男同学认为这不现实，故也排除。
答案	B

Question 24

题目定位词 / 关键词	male student; worry about; word limit; deadline; not having enough material
录音原文定位	**MAN:** ...But the problem is that our tutor has given us too much material about archaeology, so that might be challenging for us to pick out what we really need and try to condense it. **WOMAN:** What's the word limit? **MAN:** <u>She told us to write within 2000 words. That's my main concern now.</u>
题目解释	题干：男同学担心什么？ A：论文的字数限制 B：论文的截止时间 C：论文的素材不足 根据题干可知，应去找 worry about 的相似表达。在听力原文中男同学提到导师给了他们太多关于考古学的素材，可能很难找出真正需要的东西并将其浓缩，这就是男同学担心的事情。随后女同学问字数的问题，男同学回答 She told us to write within 2000 words. That's my main concern now，也就是说男同学担心素材太多了，怕不能满足字数要求。concern 对应题干中的 worry about，由此可知答案为选项 A。 选项 B 与原文表述不符，男同学表示只要把结构组织好了，赶上进度就不是问题（As long as we have organized the structure, catching up on the essay won't be a problem）。选项 C 与原文表述矛盾，男同学表示导师给了他们太多素材（our tutor has given us too much material）。
答案	A

Question 25

题目定位词 / 关键词	female student, biggest confidence, subject, presentation, writing style
录音原文定位	**WOMAN:** Well, I believe I can handle that. However, I'm a little worried about the presentation. You know, speaking in public has always been one of my nightmares. And...<u>although I have faith in our topic, which is novel and up-to-date,</u> I'm afraid that my writing style is not consistent with the academic writing style.
题目解释	题干：女同学在哪方面最有信心？ A：主旨 B：演示文稿 C：写作风格 本题问女同学在哪方面最有信心，据此应该去找 biggest confidence 的相似表达，由此可定位到女同学的话 although I have faith in our topic，faith 对应题干中的 confidence，因此答案为选项 A，subject matter 对应原文中的 topic。 选项 B 和 C 是女同学有些担心的地方（I'm a little worried about the presentation；I'm afraid that my writing style is not consistent with the academic writing style），即不是有信心的方面，故排除。
答案	A

Questions 26-30

题型： 配对题

Question 26

题目定位词 / 关键词	Archaeological Excavations in Greece
录音原文定位	MAN: Yes. The first book I read was *Archaeological Excavations in Greece*... WOMAN: Yeah, it contains lots of details, such as the description of the excavation site and a list of all the people involved, which are pretty useful. But I can't find the place where the event occurred in Chapter Two. Then I browsed the Internet to search for the place, and found that it actually doesn't exist.
题目解释	根据书名可定位至 The first book I read was *Archaeological Excavations in Greece*，女同学说找不到事件发生的地方（I can't find the place），然后在网站搜索那个地方，发现它实际上并不存在（actually doesn't exist），由此可知这本书提供了错误的位置信息，因此答案为 D。
答案	D

Question 27

题目定位词 / 关键词	Discovering Our Past
录音原文定位	WOMAN: And I also read the book *Discovering Our Past*. It introduces lots of background information about archaeological excavations, explaining the definitions of some important terms in this field.
题目解释	根据书名可定位至 And I also read the book *Discovering Our Past*，女同学说这本书介绍了大量关于考古发掘的背景信息(background information)，解释了该领域中一些重要术语的定义(explaining the definitions of some important terms in this field)，由此可知这本书系统地介绍了考古学这门学科，因此答案为 C。
答案	C

Question 28

题目定位词 / 关键词	Reading Stratigraphy
录音原文定位	MAN: It sounds that it's suitable for beginners. To be honest, I haven't read that book yet. But I've read another one called *Reading Stratigraphy*. WOMAN: I've read it, too. What impressed me most about the book is that it has a very long bibliography. MAN: About four or five pages, right? WOMAN: Five pages. I must admit that the bibliography inspired me to analyse things from different angles.

题目解释	根据书名可定位至 But I've read another one called *Reading Stratigraphy*，随后女同学说这本书给她印象最深的是它的参考书目非常长（a very long bibliography），并且后文女同学还提到这些参考书为她以不同的角度分析事物提供了灵感（inspired me to analyse things from different angles），这里的 inspired 与 useful 表达的意思相似，由此可知答案为 G。
答案	G

Question 29

题目定位词 / 关键词	*Techniques of Archaeological Excavations*
录音原文定位	**WOMAN:** ...Oh, and I highly recommend the book *Techniques of Archaeological Excavations*. I found it boring and dull at first. But later on, I indulged in the book and just couldn't put it down.
题目解释	根据书名可定位至 and I highly recommend the book *Techniques of Archaeological Excavations*，随后女同学说一开始觉得这本书很枯燥乏味，但后来沉迷于这本书 (indulged in the book)，无法放下，由此可知这本书读起来很有趣，因此答案为 A。
答案	A

Question 30

题目定位词 / 关键词	*Roman Remained in Britain*
录音原文定位	**MAN:** I felt the same way about it, actually. And I think you would like this book, too–*Roman Remained in Britain*. It's a well-organized book with a clear structure. However, one problem is that, if I recall correctly, the book doesn't mention anything about the silver bowl, which I think is an essential part in our essay.
题目解释	根据书名可定位至 And I think you would like this book, too—*Roman Remained in Britain*，随后男同学说这本书条理清晰，但没有提到关于银碗的内容（doesn't mention anything about the silver bowl），这是必不可少的部分（an essential part in our essay），由此可知这本书遗漏了一条重要信息，因此答案为 E。
答案	E

场景词汇

单词	音标	词性	释义	单词	音标	词性	释义
excavation	/ˌekskəˈveɪʃn/	n.	发掘，挖掘	burial ground		phr.	坟地
archaeologist	/ˌɑːkiˈɒlədʒɪst/	n.	考古学家	preserve	/prɪˈzɜːv/	v.	保护，维护；保持，维持
discovery	/dɪˈskʌvəri/	n.	发现，被发现的事物	pattern	/ˈpætn/	n.	图案，花样
object	/ˈɒbdʒɪkt/	n.	物体，实物	revise	/rɪˈvaɪz/	v.	修改，修订

拓展词汇

单词	音标	词性	释义	单词	音标	词性	释义
decorate	/ˈdekəreɪt/	v.	装饰，装点	strike	/straɪk/	v.	突然想到；给……印象
accompany	/əˈkʌmpəni/	v.	陪伴，陪同	spot	/spɒt/	v.	看见，注意到
ownership	/ˈəʊnəʃɪp/	n.	所有权	ambitious	/æmˈbɪʃəs/	adj.	宏大的，野心勃勃的
sort out		phr.	把……分门别类	slide	/slaɪd/	n.	幻灯片
condense	/kənˈdens/	v.	压缩，简缩	nightmare	/ˈnaɪtmeə(r)/	n.	噩梦；可怕的经历
consistent	/kənˈsɪstənt/	adj.	始终如一的，一贯的	novel	/ˈnɒvl/	adj.	新颖的
omit	/əˈmɪt/	v.	忽视，忽略	subject matter		phr.	主题，题材，主要内容

Test 6 解析

Part 4　*Questions 31-40*

场景介绍

主题场景	人文社科		考查题型	笔记填空题 + 选择题（单项）
主旨大意	一项关于 13 世纪初当地农村生活的研究项目报告			

逐题精讲

Questions 31-36

　题型：**笔记填空题**

Question 31

题目定位词 / 关键词	Research information obtained from; archives; Internet
录音原文定位	I derived my information from a variety of sources——most of it from archives held in the museum and some very valuable information from the Internet.
题目解释	根据题干可知，空格处应该填写一个名词或形容词，用以形容 archives（档案），同时它也是获得研究信息的某种渠道之一，与 Internet 并列。由小标题的信息可以定位至 I derived my information from a variety of sources，紧接着男士说大部分都来自博物馆的档案（archives held in the museum），有些重要的信息来自互联网（some very valuable information from the Internet）。由于第 31 题下面的已知信息为 the Internet，正好对应原文中的 some very valuable information from the Internet，因此 and 之前的信息就是空格处的答案，archives 原词重现，空格处填写的单词为 museum。
答案	museum

Question 32

题目定位词 / 关键词	a; librarians
录音原文定位	The librarians there helped me track down a map which proved extremely informative for the project.
题目解释	根据题干可知，空格处应该填写一个单数可数名词，与 librarians 有关，它也是获得研究信息的一个渠道，由此可定位至 Finally, quite late on in my research, I contacted the city library。紧接着男士说图书管理员帮他找到了一张地图，track down 对应题干中的 found，句中单数可数名词为 map，由此可知答案为 map。
答案	map

Question 33

题目定位词 / 关键词	farms; ditch; for
录音原文定位	An average household farmed between ten and thirty acres of land and most homes had deep ditches around them which were dug not for drainage, but in order to provide protection.
题目解释	根据题干可知，空格处应该填写一个名词或动名词，表示农场周围的沟渠的作用。根据 ditch 可定位至 An average household farmed between ten and thirty acres of land and most homes had deep ditches around them, which 引导的从句引出 deep ditches 的用途，重点在转折词 but 后，in order to 对应题干中的 for，所以答案为 protection。
答案	protection

Question 34

题目定位词 / 关键词	richer people; bought pottery and spices; indicated by; different types of
录音原文定位	We are able to deduce this from the number of different kinds of shops selling these types of products in settlements in the area.
题目解释	根据题干可知，空格处应该填写一个名词，作为有钱人购买陶器和香料的依据，由此可定位至 the main purchases for wealthier households were pottery for cooking purposes and also spices，后文男士说 We are able to deduce this from the number of different kinds of shops selling... 其中 deduce from（推测）对应题干中的 indicated by，different kinds of 对应题干中的 different types of，由此可知答案为 shops。
答案	shops

Question 35

题目定位词 / 关键词	peas and beans; the soil
录音原文定位	These latter were extensively grown because they fertilized the land and made anything planted after them grow well.
题目解释	根据题干可知，空格处应该填写一个主动语态的动词，动作的主语是 peas and beans，由此可定位至 Turning now to the crops, these were mainly cereals and legumes, peas and beans，紧接着男士说 These latter were extensively grown because they fertilized the land, these latter 指代前一句中的 peas and beans，land 对应题干中的 soil，由此可知答案为 fertilized。
答案	fertilized

Question 36

题目定位词 / 关键词	chaff; guarded against; disease and attacks
录音原文定位	Serial seats, for example, were covered in a thick case of chaff which meant they were protected against diseases such as rust and also against assaults by birds.
题目解释	根据题干可知，空格处应该填写一个名词，表示谷壳（chaff）的作用——抵御来自疾病和某物的攻击，由此可定位至 Serial seats, for example, were covered in a thick case of chaff，关键信息在 which 引导的定语从句 which meant they were protected against diseases such as rust and also against assaults by birds 中，其中 protected against 对应题干中的 guarded against，assaults 对应题干中的 attacks，由此可知答案为 birds。
答案	birds

Questions 37-40

题型：选择题（单项）

Question 37

题目定位词 / 关键词	Crop mixing; effective; because; harvesting much quicker; guaranteed yields; kept the soil in an excellent condition
录音原文定位	It means that if the weather is unsuitable for one crop, it is usually better for the other. This way, a reasonable harvest is ensured.
题目解释	题干：混合种植作物行之有效的原因是什么？ A：收获比之前更快 B：即使遇到天气问题也能保证产量 C：使土壤保持良好的状态 由关键词可定位至 Firstly, one farming practice which was being introduced at this time was crop mixing，接下来先介绍 crop mixing 的使用场景，随后说如果天气不适合一种作物，通常对另一种作物更好，就能确保合理的收成。由此可知，即使有天气问题，仍可保证产量，因此答案为 B，guaranteed 对应原文中的 ensured，yields 对应原文中的 harvest。 选项 A 与原文表述矛盾，原文说的是 in conditions where crops are harvested slowly by hand，故排除。选项 C 在原文中未提及，故也排除。
答案	B

Question 38

题目定位词 / 关键词	heavy plough; changes to; seeds planted; animals; shape of the fields
录音原文定位	So it was better to change from short to very long thin fields.
题目解释	题干：重型犁的引入带来什么改变？ A：所种植种子类型的变化 B：用于犁田的动物类型的变化 C：田地形状的变化 根据 heavy plough 首先可定位至 Another innovation...was the introduction of the heavy plough，接着提到了 heavy plough 的一些特点，肯定了其给农业带来的变化（This brought long lasting changes to farming）。接着介绍了具体的变化，说因为重型犁的机动性差（less maneuverable），拉犁的动物不能轻易改变方向，因此耕种的田从短的薄田变成长的薄田（change from short to very long thin fields），由此可知给田地的形状带来了改变，因此答案为 C。 选项 A 与原文表述不符，原文说让种子能更稳定地播种（enabled seeds to be planted securely），不是种子类型的改变。 选项 B 在原文中有所提及，通常是 oxen，有时是 heavy horses (the draft animals, usually oxen at this time, but sometimes heavy horses,))，但并未发生改变，故排除。
答案	C

Question 39

题目定位词 / 关键词	innovation; windmills; new shape of sail; move the sails; removed more easily
录音原文定位	What was introduced at this time was fixing the sails onto a post which could easily be maneuvered to put the sails in the position to make the most of the available wind.
题目解释	题干：风力磨坊有什么创新之处？ A：引入了一种新形状的帆 B：人们可以将帆移到迎风的位置 C：帆比以前更容易移走 本题问风力磨坊有何创新之处，可定位至 windmills of all shapes and sizes that had been used for... 这里首先提到了 windmills。随后一句 What was introduced at this time 对应题干中的 innovation，因此这里是本题答案出处。创新之处是 fixing the sails onto a post which could easily be maneuvered to put the sails in the position to make the most of the available wind，意思是把帆固定在一根很容易操纵的柱子上，从而将帆放在适当的位置，以充分利用可用的风力，由此可知答案为 B。 选项 A 在原文中未提及，故排除。选项 C 为原文 could easily be maneuvered 的干扰信息，could easily be maneuvered 的对象是 post，不是 sail，故也排除。
答案	B

Question 40

题目定位词 / 关键词	Small-holders; better crop yields; because; only; effective farming practices; suited to the soil; free labour
录音原文定位	But this was highly labor intensive. This suited the poor smallholders because they had family members to draw on to do the work.
题目解释	题干：小农户为什么比富裕的农民获得的作物产量更高？ A：只有他们知道高效的农耕方式 B：他们种植的作物非常适合土壤 C：他们能轻易地获得大量的免费劳动力 根据关键词首先可定位至 poorer farmers with small holdings were actually beginning to produce higher yields their land than their rich lords and masters。本句提到了题干的信息，但具体的原因在下文给出，即劳动密集型（labor intensive）种植更适合较为贫困的小农，因为他们有家庭成员来做这份工作（they had family members to draw on to do the work），由此可知答案为 C。 选项 A 与原文表述相矛盾，原文说的是贫农和富农都知道（Both groups knew of good new practices of exhaustive weeding and more intensive planting），故排除。 选项 B 在原文中未提及，故也排除。
答案	C

场景词汇

单词	音标	词性	释义	单词	音标	词性	释义
investigate	/ɪnˈvestɪgeɪt/	v.	调查，研究	archive	/ˈɑːkaɪv/	n.	存档材料，档案
ditch	/dɪtʃ/	n.	沟渠，壕沟	drainage	/ˈdreɪnɪdʒ/	n.	排出的水，污水
pottery	/ˈpɒtəri/	n.	陶器	herb	/hɜːb/	n.	药草，香草
settlements	/ˈsetlmənt/	n.	定居点，聚居地	fertilize	/ˈfɜːtəlaɪz/	v.	使肥沃
genetic modification		phr.	基因转变	chaff	/tʃæf/	v.	糠；谷壳
machinery	/məˈʃiːnəri/	n.	机器，机械（尤指大型机械）	plough	/plaʊ/	n.	犁
draft animal		phr.	役畜（拉重物的牲畜）	windmill	/ˈwɪndmɪl/	n.	风力磨坊；风车
weeding	/ˈwiːdɪŋ/	n.	除草	labor intensive		phr.	劳动密集型

拓展词汇

单词	音标	词性	释义	单词	音标	词性	释义
derive from		*phr.*	源自，来自	track down		*phr.*	查出，找到
informative	/ɪnˈfɔːmətɪv/	*adj.*	提供有用信息的	unrest	/ʌnˈrest/	*n.*	不安；动荡的局面
indication	/ˌɪndɪˈkeɪʃn/	*n.*	标示；象征，暗示	deduce	/dɪˈdjuːs/	*v.*	推断，演绎
extensively	/ɪkˈstensɪvli/	*adv.*	广阔地；广泛地	nitrogen	/ˈnaɪtrədʒən/	*n.*	氮
by trial and error		*phr.*	反复试验，不断摸索	assault	/əˈsɔːlt/	*n.*	袭击，攻击
undergo	/ˌʌndəˈgəʊ/	*v.*	经历，经受	unsuitable	/ʌnˈsuːtəbl/	*adj.*	不适合的，不适宜的
maneuverable	/məˈnuːvərəbl/	*adj.*	容易操作的	exhaustive	/ɪgˈzɔːstɪv/	*adj.*	详尽的，彻底的

03

Section 3

录音文本

Test 1

Part 1

WOMAN: Hello, thanks for calling the Amateur Dramatic Association. This is assistant Jane speaking. How can I help you?

MAN: Hi there. I'm really interested in drama, so I'm ringing to enquire for more details of the association.

WOMAN: Glad to hear that, Sir. What do you want to know about?

MAN: Well, first of all, I wonder where you usually rehearse.

WOMAN: We've posted an address on our website. It's 117/155 Green Street, but that's our mailing address. Actually, our rehearsals take place in the Club (**Q1**) House.

MAN: That's great! It's not far from my place. You see, I'm thinking about joining a drama club. Do you have any vacancies at the moment?

WOMAN: Yes, we do. We've been recruiting members recently. You don't need to have any previous experience, but we're particularly in need of actors and male (**Q2**) singers.

MAN: I see. I think I'll make a good actor. I've participated in many performances since high school. Do you have any special requirements?

WOMAN: Yes, do you have a car? It's better if you can drive (**Q3**), because you know, for each play, there're always many stage props needed. The association really needs someone to help transport them.

MAN: That won't be a problem. I got my driving license years ago and I bought my own car two years ago.

WOMAN: Sounds great. It seems like you're the person we're looking for.

MAN: Haha. What about the hours? I'm afraid I won't be available on Thursdays because I have private tutoring lessons that day. I hope that's okay for you.

WOMAN: Don't worry at all. Our routine meetings are on Tuesday (**Q4**) every week. We start at 6 o'clock in the evening and end at 8 o'clock.

MAN: Oh, that's a relief. So, you don't open on Thursdays, am I right?

WOMAN: Exactly. Please rest assured.

MAN: Okay. I also wanna know, do we have to practice on holidays? Will there be any time off?

WOMAN: Sure, there will. The Club will be closed for 2 weeks in August (**Q5**), so you don't have to rehearse during that time.

MAN: Awesome!

MAN: Could you tell me more about the membership? What exactly does it include?

WOMAN: Of course. Our members are pretty close to each other. We have a lot of group activities every year, including an annual dinner (**Q6**).

MAN: That sounds interesting. I'd love to make some new friends. How much is your membership fee?

WOMAN: Normally it's 40 pounds and 60 pence for each member, but if you currently don't have a job or have already retired, we will charge you only 25 (**Q7**) pounds. We used to have 10% off instead, but now we've increased our discount, which is 15 pounds less than the original price. Elderly people over 60 years old can also enjoy our discount on the membership fee.

MAN: That's a pretty fair price. It seems like your members cover a wide range of age groups. Are there any children in the association, too? My 15-year-old niece is also quite into theatre. Perhaps she could also become part of the Club?

WOMAN: That's right. We pursue diversity in our association and welcome people of different ages from all walks of life to join us, but I'm afraid we have an age limit for children. We only accept minors aged 16 (**Q8**) and younger.

MAN: That's all right. What kind of plays do you have then?

WOMAN: Well, for the classics, we have Shakespeare, of course. Besides that, our members mainly focus on modern plays (**Q9**).

MAN: That's great. Could you tell me more about your performances?

WOMAN: No problem. Apart from the normal plays mentioned above, it's also our tradition to host a charity show every Christmas, from which all the money gathered will be donated to children's hospitals (**Q10**).

MAN: That's really nice of you to do that. What should I do to register for membership?

WOMAN: Firstly, I'm going to need you to give me some personal information...

Test 1
录音文本

Part 2

Hello, everyone. My name is Tom, and I'm the administrator of our community. Thank you all for coming to the community meeting. Today, I'm here to introduce our newly-built Waste Recycling Centre, which, like its name suggests, helps us to deal with garbage more efficiently. Hopefully, the environment in our community will become better.

As you can see, many garbage cans have been placed in some fixed areas, which will help you to recycle certain waste that is difficult to deal with, such as paint. In order to be more environmental-friendly, I suggest you to buy just the amount of paint you need (*Q11*). If you cannot use it up, please throw it into the dustbin. Paints of all types, including metal paint, will be accepted and sent for re-use in the community.

The collection vehicles may travel different routes on some occasions, so the time your bin and recycling are collected may vary. The collection schedule can be found in the customer service centre (*Q12*). If you have problems finding it, you can ask the information desk for help, which is on the right of the front gate. The receptionist will show you the way there. There's one thing to remind you about. If you are a close observer, you would have noticed there is a warning sign for you to keep the garbage lid closed at all times, even during the collection period for some health and safety reasons.

Also, please make sure that your bins are away from the roadside since traffic accidents may be caused by the waste bin falling down and rolling onto the road. In the normal course of things, trailers will come from the parking lot, so you should leave one metre's space (*Q13*), allowing trailers to pass between dustbins and collect garbage.

Aside from the placement of dustbins, another thing you shouldn't forget is to remove the caps and lids on bottles and containers(*Q14*) before recycling them. The cap is made from a different kind of plastic than the bottle, and it must be separated before they can be processed because they have different melting points. Otherwise, the water inside will affect the squashing process.

You will see that bins of more than one colour are placed in the area. I understand that you may have problems identifying which category your waste belongs to, and consequently which container you should throw your waste into. So, next I'll explain this to you in detail.

The yellow bin currently collects recyclable material from almost 96% of households. Paper and cards(*Q15*) are accepted, such as newspapers, magazines, catalogues, contents of unwanted mail, telephone directories, yellow pages, cardboard and envelopes.

On the right side of the yellow bin is a white bin, where you can dispose domestic white goods like refrigerators and washing machines. Even if they are old or damaged, some spare parts(**Q16**) can still be put back into service after processing, so please keep them separated from scrap metal.

Opposite to the white bin, there is a red bin. It is for small household batteries and batteries from cars (**Q17**). Lithium batteries cannot be disposed here because they belong to the hazardous waste category, which refers to the rubbish that are flammable, toxic, corrosive and reactive.

Next is the zone for glass. Glass is a very useful material for our packaging because it is very easy to recycle. Glass can be recycled completely and indefinitely without losing its original quality and property. Glass containers that can be put in the glass recycling bin include bottles of any colour, bottles for wine, beer and spirits, and food jars such as sauces, jam and baby food. Remember to place the glass item in the correct coloured bin – the brown bin is for glass with no colour (**Q18**), the green bin is for brown glass, and green and blue glass should go into the blue bin.

And the last part is for cartridge recycling. Toner recycling is the latest raw material to make its way into the recycling chain and is important because the materials used to make ink and toner cartridges can be harmful to human health and the environment. Fortunately, nearly 100% of printer cartridge materials can be recycled. This greatly reduces airborne pollutants. You can drop your printer cartridge (**Q19**) off at the purple bin and all types of toner cartridges will be accepted there, including ink (**Q20**).

Well, that's basically everything for our waste recycling centre. Thank you all for listening. Are there any questions?

Test 1
录音文本

Part 3

SIMON: Hello, Anna. This is Simon speaking. May I talk to you for a few minutes?

ANNA: No problem. Nice to hear from you, Simon. What's the matter?

SIMON: Actually... I'm quite confused about what course to choose in the next semester and I wanna ask you for some advice.

ANNA: Sure, I'd be glad to help. Any preferences you have now?

SIMON: There are too many courses, and I... I have no idea where to start.

ANNA: No worries. What about starting from your choices in your freshman year? What curriculum do you have now?

SIMON: Well... I chose Literature at the beginning of this semester, but I'm considering whether to change it into Tourism Management in the next year.

ANNA: Why? I think that Literature is pretty interesting. I still remember I looked forward to attending this class every time.

SIMON: Yes, it sure is. But you know... I plan to study overseas in my senior year. And this course can help me work around the world, especially in New Zealand (**Q21**).

ANNA: I understand. Or maybe you can regard it as a plan B. Mm... let me see what else might be helpful to you. How about Finance or Economics? These sorts of courses can be useful wherever you go.

SIMON: That's a good idea. But the problem is I have flipped through the course handout of Finance, and found it has many chapters that coincide with other courses I had. As for Economics...well, although it may allow me to have access to some office work, I still think it is boring and dull as a course (**Q22**), because I already learned it in high school and I have no interest in it.

ANNA: Then things have reached a stalemate.

SIMON: Oh, I also saw that Quantitative Analysis was on the course list, but I heard that the final exam of the course is very difficult. Have you ever taken this class?

ANNA: No, it's too challenging for me. The benefit is that you will get more credits than other courses. But, of course, that's under the premise of successfully passing the final exam. All in all, it's up to you, as it's an elective course (**Q23**).

SIMON: I see. Thanks for all the information, and I will think it over. By the way, what courses do you wanna choose for your next semester?

ANNA: I'm going to take a Foreign Language Course. At first, I thought learning a foreign language would help enhance my travelling experiences. However, unfortunately, my travel plans have gone up the spout.

SIMON: So why don't you change to another kind of course?

ANNA: Actually I made this decision for another reason. I'm aiming at engaging in business after graduation since I find it useful (**Q24**). So I chose Chinese and Japanese, to be more specific, to facilitate business communication.

SIMON:　Right. That sounds helpful. Are the lectures given by Professor Smith?

ANNA:　Yes, he is also responsible for a course in the first year.

SIMON:　Oh, I'm having his course now and I really enjoy it. You can feel that he has a great passion for the class (**Q25**).

ANNA:　I agree. He always introduces all aspects of the research topic, so students will definitely gain a lot as long as they listen carefully. But that can also turn into a problem. His lecture is always teacher-centered. Students should be motivated to think critically (**Q26**).

SIMON:　Yeah, and as an art student, the analytical method adapted in his paper is too complex for me to apply.

SIMON:　I think I need to take other courses into account.

ANNA:　Wait a minute. I'm looking for the course list of our major. Here it is. Oh, I forgot Communication 1.

SIMON:　What's the course mainly about?

ANNA:　It helps you to overcome fear and deliver speeches smoothly (**Q27**), like how to organize the structure of your speech.

SIMON:　That's an important skill for our future work.

ANNA:　Yep, and there is Psychology.

SIMON:　I'm quite interested in it. Will this course teach us things about people's mental activities?

ANNA:　It will cover some of it. Well, the most practical part of it is Psychology promotes team cohesion, especially in a big group (**Q28**).

SIMON:　Sounds amazing. How does it work?

ANNA:　Well, it gives you a better understanding of people's thinking patterns and how to be more persuasive as well.

SIMON:　I see there is Interpretation. Is it similar to Communication 1?

ANNA:　Not really. It focuses on the conflicts in our daily life or work. For example, you can learn how to reduce the problems in collaborating with co-workers (**Q29**).

SIMON:　Is there any course related to culture? You know, New Zealand is quite different from us. It would be better if I can learn about some of its special features in advance.

ANNA:　Then I'd recommend Communication 3. It guides us to notice the differences in cultures, which I believe could help us effectively deal with disputes brought by them (**Q30**).

SIMON:　Great! Thanks, Anna. You've really helped me a lot!

Part 4

The next lectures in this current series will deal with various aspects of marine ecology, or how the various forms of sea life relate to each other. And today I'm going to talk about the fortunes of a type of seaweed called kelp.

In the past few years, scientists have been coming up with formulae or equations for calculating how marine life is affected by natural events such as hurricanes, or by human activity, such as pollution or fishing. And the more information they can feed into these equations, the better. Now some of the predictions that were made initially turned out to be highly inaccurate, and it was suspected that this was due to insufficient historical data being available (**Q31**). So when a team of international scientists recently set out to reevaluate the state of various coastal ecosystems from Australia to Alaska, they were concerned to increase reliability by collecting as much of this kind of data as possible (**Q31**).

And when the extra dimension was included, the findings of the team were startling. Their studies demonstrated that there has always been a complex interaction between animals and plants living in our seas, between the top predators and the grazers and grassy plains of the ocean floors.

We now know much more about what happens when humans intervene in this system (**Q32**). We know that playing with nature's ecosystems is extremely risky. You remove just one species of animal and it can have an impact on the whole system, often in an entirely unpredictable way.

Let's look, first of all, at some of the findings relating to the kelp forests of Alaska. From the ocean shore, these look rather uninspiring, just piles of seaweed apparently floating on the surface. But when you dive down into them, they are incredible. They are these great jungles of greenery stretching as much as a hundred feet from the sea bed all the way to the surface. And they're one of the most productive ecosystems in the world. They are full of wildlife and they are important nursery grounds for many of the fish we eat.

In Alaska, a team of scientists carefully pieced together the chain of events behind the fluctuating fortunes of the kelp forests. The main characters in this story were sea urchins which feed on kelp and sea otters which prey on the sea urchins. Sea otters were abundant in that system for three to five million years. And then somewhere between two and a half thousand to four thousand years ago when early people first occupied that region, the otter population began to decline. And it probably declined as a consequence of over hunting. However, the declines were relatively small in scale at that time and localized probably around village sites (**Q33**). So early humans had hunted the otters. This left more sea urchins to graze the kelp forests, clearing great patches of it.

For thousands of years, this occurred only near native settlements until the Europeans arrived. In the mid-seventeen hundreds, the Alaskan Waters were discovered by the Bering Expedition and that set off the North Pacific fur trade (**Q34**). And as a consequence of that, otter populations were rapidly depleted (**Q35**) to very low levels across the whole region. And that in turn caused an explosion of sea urchin population (**Q36**) and thus a collapse of the kelp forests (**Q37**). So when humans wiped out the top predator, grazers took over and over-grazed the kelp forests until they were devastated. Then in the early nineteen hundreds before the Alaskan sea otters were completely wiped out, they became a protected species (**Q38**). And as the otter population built up again, sea urchin numbers declined. So for much of the twentieth century, kelp forests recovered and began to flourish again, although they were nothing like the vibrant ecosystem they had once been.

In some ways it was like English woodlands where large predators like wolves and bears have been replaced by voles and shrews. But unfortunately, the story doesn't end there. The roller coaster ride of the kelp ecosystem was far from over. In the late twentieth century, the unlucky sea otters began to decline again. Because this time they were being eaten by killer whales (**Q39**). So scientists set out to find out why killer whales had suddenly changed their diets. And they have come to a tentative conclusion: the killer whales had been eating young sea lions and harbor seals, and perhaps northern fur seals. But when these animals declined, they switched to eating otters. This was an unprecedented event that scientists believed had never happened before in history. And by about 1996, otter populations had been devastated. So as a result of this, the kelp forests can be expected to decline (**Q40**) again since the sea urchin numbers are no longer controlled by the otters. And so the cycle continues.

On the other side of the continent in May...

Test 2

Part 1

MAN: Welcome Madam, how may I help you?

WOMAN: Hello. I've called before. I'm hoping you can help me lose some weight.

MAN: Sure! That's what we do here, isn't it? Now I just need you to give me some personal information so I can fill out the form.

WOMAN: No problem.

MAN: Alright, let's start with your name, please.

WOMAN: My name is Lily Swan.

MAN: Li-ly Swan. And, what's your current job?

WOMAN: Now I'm a nurse (*Q1*) and I am working in a hospital, but I plan to be a teacher one day, so I'm working on that.

MAN: That's great. I'll just put "nurse" down here, and if you change your job in the future, we can update your information anytime.

WOMAN: Okay.

MAN: And uh, could you tell me your phone number so we can get a hold of you?

WOMAN: Yes, my number is 0407 686 121 (*Q2*).

MAN: Got it. Now I need to know about your height and weight so I know where to start.

WOMAN: Sure. I'm 165 cm tall and I weigh 70 kg.

MAN: Okay. What about your general health? I have to know if you are currently suffering from any problems before I can design a training scheme for you.

WOMAN: Well, I think overall I'm a healthy person. Oh, but I've been having these headaches (*Q3*) quite often. Sometimes it really kills me.

MAN: I see. A lot of people also contract the flu easily during the flu season. Do you have the same problem?

WOMAN: No, I'm alright. I seldom catch the flu, but I do suffer from colds (*Q4*) from time to time.

MAN: Alright. Do you have any allergies then?

WOMAN: Um, about that, I used to have an allergy to milk, but I've gradually outgrown it. Now I find myself allergic to seafood (*Q5*).

MAN: Okay. Is that all I need to know about? Do you have any other things troubling you?

WOMAN: Well, lately I also have sore eyes (*Q6*) quite often. Perhaps it's because I work long

03

hours and get too tired.

MAN:　　Don't worry. I'll keep it in mind.

WOMAN:　That's great.

. . . .

MAN:　　Now we can start discussing our exercise plan. Do you have any particular kind of sports that you like?

WOMAN:　Um, not really.

MAN:　　That's alright. Let me think, why don't we try having a brisk walk on Monday? It's very relaxing and should be easy to start with.

WOMAN:　Sounds great.

MAN:　　How long do you think you can keep going each time?

WOMAN:　I think, maybe 20 minutes.

MAN:　　Why don't we set the bar higher? Let's say, 30 (**Q7**) minutes at the beginning, and then after a few weeks, we can step it up to 45 minutes.

WOMAN:　Okay, I think I can manage that. We can have the walk in the school square.

MAN:　　Well, the school is fine, but isn't it a bit boring? Why don't we walk in a park (**Q8**)? Is there any nearby?

WOMAN:　Yeah, I agree. Walking in a park is certainly much more interesting. There is a local park not far from my place.

MAN:　　Excellent.

WOMAN:　Should I bring anything with me during the walk?

MAN:　　Sure. You'd better wear a pair of trainers for the long walk or your feet might get sore or even get hurt.

WOMAN:　You're right. And when are we going to exercise? In the morning?

MAN:　　That's right, so you should probably bring something to block the sun.

WOMAN:　Okay. I'll wear my hat then.

MAN:　　Good. Then on Tuesday, how about some yoga (**Q9**) for 90 minutes?

WOMAN:　No problem. I like yoga. May I ask, where we are going to do this?

MAN:　　The sports centre (**Q10**) is open. We can do yoga in there.

WOMAN:　Good idea.

MAN:　　Remember to wear something comfortable and bring a mat.

WOMAN:　Sure. I'll just wear my loose clothes then.

Test 2
录音文本

Part 2

Welcome to the Heritage Trust information line. This is a recorded message. You will not be charged for this call.

The Heritage Trust is a charity which exists to preserve old properties of national importance. It owns and maintains 49 of these properties throughout the country, 47 of which are open to the public. The entrance fee varies from property to property. But by becoming a member of the trust you can enjoy many benefits including free entrance to all its properties. We offer several different types of membership. The individual membership is our most popular with an annual cost of twenty nine pounds fifty (*Q11*). But we also have a senior plan and that's available for individuals who are 58 years and above(*Q12*), and is at the special rate of twenty one pounds twenty per year. Obviously we would not require you to produce proof of age every time you visit a property, but we do ask that when you register for a senior membership, you send us a photocopy of your passport (*Q13*). This is all we require for proof of age.

Another type we offer is group membership. Many schools and other educational parties like to take advantage of this special rate, but it can also be used for clubs or family groups as you wish. The only requirement is that the group consists of more than twelve people. The total cost is 190 pounds and can be used at any time throughout the week including weekends. But unfortunately we are unable to allow visits on National Holidays (*Q14*) under this plan. We are very sorry that we have recently had to introduce this condition because crowding can cause damage to our properties, especially on these very popular days.

So how can you become a member. We offer two different ways to apply for membership. Of course, you can join at any trust property simply by filling in a form in the office. Any one of our staff would be happy to help you do this. And you can also join by post. Please write to the HT Membership Department. PO Box six five four seven. And that's in Beanham. Spelled B-E-A-N-H-A-M (*Q15*), which is in Devonshire, PL twenty three nine PU (*Q16*). Enclose a check for the relevant amount and send your name, address and contact telephone number.

Unfortunately, we are not yet able to offer Internet joining facilities. Upon joining us you will receive a welcome pack which has a wealth of useful information about the trust and its properties. It includes directions to all HD properties(*Q17*). Often the properties are in very out of the way places so don't lose the directions. The pack also gives full information about property opening times as well as details about any special shows at each site.

We are now able to guarantee that all heritage trust properties offer the following facilities to visitors: car parking, which is free to all visiting the house(*Q18*)—just keep your entrance ticket or membership card and show it on exit; a special heritage trust shop selling a wide range of top quality merchandise; a restaurant with particular emphasis on locally produced food (**Q19**) and guided tours in four European languages. For up-to-date data information, each house now has its own website (**Q20**). Just do a search under the name of the house. We are committed to providing...

Part 3

Joel:	Hi, Dr. Owens. Are you busy now? I wonder if you could give me some advice on my research paper.
Dr. Owens:	Sure, what's your topic?
Joel:	I'm thinking about studying the influences of government policies and new technologies on farming.
Dr. Owens:	Agriculture? That's interesting. Have you decided on which country's situation you want to talk about?
Joel:	Yes, I will mainly focus on Australia. Right, maybe I should point that out in the title.
Dr. Owens:	Hmm, perhaps it'd be better if you could carry out a case study of a certain area and then narrow it down to several particular farms. Specify the place in your title so it won't seem too general (**Q21**).
Joel:	That's a great idea. I can investigate the different types of farming in an eastern town and interview the farmers.
Dr. Owens:	Certainly. How do you plan to interview them? On the phone or face-to-face?
Joel:	I prefer the latter method.
Dr. Owens:	Why is that? Is that because you want to see the farms yourself?
Joel:	A face-to-face interview does allow me to do that, but that's not really my intention. From my experience, people don't like to discuss serious things on the phone, so they usually cut their answers short and sometimes even don't say what they really mean. By talking directly to the farmers, I'm more likely to get a complete response from them (**Q22**).
Dr. Owens:	That makes sense. Also, when you're looking into their eyes, it's easier to make them feel closer to you. You may even end up being friends with them.
Joel:	Haha, that's true.
Dr. Owens:	And you mentioned new technologies. When you're in the field, how exactly will you find out their influences on the farmers?
Joel:	I guess I'll just show them some pictures of modern farming, and then ask them how they feel about them.
Dr. Owens:	Well, pictures can be vivid and direct, but I'd say it's better to avoid being so specific. Similarly, instead of giving them a questionnaire with leading questions, you can just start with some general questions (**Q23**). This can help you avoid influencing them and allow them to answer the question in their own way that reveals their true thoughts.
Joel:	You're right. I'll change my method then (**Q23**).
Dr. Owens:	You also mentioned the government's role in agriculture. What information have you gathered so far?

Joel:　　　Yes, I've done some research online trying to find out what policies have been made in this area. From what I've learnt, the government is actually quite supportive of the agricultural industry, though the results are not very satisfying. The investment in farming has been on the rise these years and they also encourage the farmers to introduce new farming equipment and technologies.

Dr. Owens:　Right, these are all measures that try to increase the total grain output, but despite their good intentions, they forget to address the real problems and desires of farmers in face of the new changes (**Q24**).

Joel:　　　I couldn't agree more. Based on what I've read, many of them actually wish to try out some new farming equipment and technologies, but end up flinching back because of how complicated they appear(**Q25**). And since they don't really understand their value, they consider it a mere waste of money. They would rather work with the whole family or employ some workers instead to increase the output.

Dr. Owens:　That's a shame, isn't it? More guidance should be given to the farmers on how to keep pace with the new era. I remember reading a research paper by a group of Australian experts. According to them, the vast majority of farmers are, in fact, willing to work with the government and adapt to the modern way. However, most of them don't know how to gather information and usually rush into making some wrong adjustments that produce bad results (**Q26**).

Joel:　　　Exactly. This will only further undermine their confidence in any new investments. Instead of putting their money in some promising farming technologies or trusting someone professional to handle their money wisely, they tend to just save it away and never touch it again. That way they will feel much safer...

Joel:　　　So, Dr. Owens, here is a booklist for agriculture that I downloaded online. I feel that I have a lot to catch up in this area, but I'm afraid I don't have time for all of these books. Could you give me some advice on which ones to give up?

Dr. Owens:　Sure. Not every book is worth reading. Let me see...Well, firstly, I wouldn't recommend *An Overview of Agricultural Development in Human Society*. Though many say it's a must-read if you want to learn about the history of agriculture, it's really dull and many students won't make it to the second chapter (**Q27**).

Joel:　　　Tell me about it! I tried reading it several times but always gave up halfway.

Dr. Owens:　And, you can remove this one from your list—*How Do Government Policies Affect Farmers*. It has several interesting ideas regarding the influences of the government, but the whole book is a mess. The author tries to appear smart by using a lot of big words and jargons, but in fact the content of each section is loosely put together and the logic between them just doesn't hold (**Q28**).

Joel: Got it. That sounds terrible. Any others?

Dr. Owens: Well, *New Technologies in Modern Farming*, this one definitely has to go.

Joel: Why is that?

Dr. Owens: I've read the book before, and to my surprise, there were many mistakes in the content, like the chapter introducing farm automation (**Q29**).

Joel: Whoa, I'm lucky I came to you first. Otherwise, I could've been misled by it.

Dr. Owens: That's right. Oh, and this one, *How to Take Farming to the Next Level*. You can skip it. It used to be one of the required readings and even the textbook for those majoring in agriculture, but that was two decades ago. The examples it uses are too old and some analyses don't apply to the current situation (**Q30**).

Joel: I see. Is that all?

Dr. Owens: Yes, you should finish the rest of the list if you want to conduct an in-depth investigation.

Joel: Of course. Thanks a lot, Dr. Owens. You've really helped me save a lot of time...

Part 4

Good morning everyone, welcome to our lecture. Today we're going to talk about African clawed frogs. They are the oldest kind of tailless amphibian creatures with a habitat in central and southern Africa. That's why they're known as African. Their scientific name is Xenopus laevis. African clawed frogs are renowned for their use as a model organism for a variety of biological and biochemical studies, but let's start with some general descriptions of them first.

African clawed frogs have very smooth (*Q31*) skin, which can change its color to adapt to the environment. In their natural habitats, you may find them with different colors – monochrome light green, brown, or with gray or black streaks on their back. Their skin is covered with thick mucus which forms a layer of film. It can prevent excess water from entering the body and thus serves as a way of protection (*Q32*). Some may wonder how big the frogs are. Well, there can be huge differences depending on their sex. Male frogs are much smaller than the female ones. An adult female frog is about 4 inches long, whereas a male frog only measures 2 inches, which means it's half (*Q33*) as long as the female one.

As their name suggests, African clawed frogs are indigenous to Africa. You may find this species of aquatic frogs in all sorts of water in sub-Saharan Africa. Nevertheless, they prefer to live in still (*Q34*) water, which means they don't like running streams and you're more likely to see them in the stagnant (*Q34*) ponds or lakes. African clawed frogs are very tolerant to changes in the environment and will survive in almost any body of water. For example, they can live in water that contains a high level of salt (*Q35*). However, although they're hardy creatures, they're very sensitive to metal. Any presence of metal ions could kill them. So you have to be extra careful about what you discharge into the water. Also, you should never use a metal container to transport them in captive care. Though they usually live in the water, during droughts, they can also burrow into the mud (*Q36*), becoming dormant for up to a year.

Adult frogs become scavengers, eating living, dead or dying arthropods and other pieces of organic waste in the water, including aquatic insect larvae, water insects, crustaceans, small fish, tadpoles, worms and freshwater snails. They rely on their acute sense of smell (*Q37*) and extremely sensitive fingers to locate and catch their prey. They also have a lateral line system on both sides of the body, which gives them the ability to sense movements and vibrations in the water and help detect the prey. In the feeding process, since African clawed frogs do not have tongues, they use their forelimbs and a special pump (*Q38*) to press food into their mouths for consumption.

Although the frogs are native to Africa, they've been gradually introduced to many other parts of the world, especially the United States. A lot of Americans consider them a new, fun, and exciting pet to add to their aquariums and they are also used extensively as laboratory research animals. However, though they're popular in the US, in some states like California, African clawed frogs multiply rapidly and act like an invasive species that negatively affects other species in the freshwater ecosystems. That's why they are treated as a type of pest (*Q39*) in these places. African clawed frogs have been particularly useful for studying very early events, such as the formation of the neural plate which develops into the nervous system. One reason is that the female frogs are prolific egg layers, producing between 500 and 2000 eggs per mating, which takes place several times a year. What's more, the embryos are transparent, making it easy to observe their development at all stages. One of the most significant protections of African clawed frogs against their ever-changing environment are the compounds secreted by their skin, such as some mucus with antibiotic (*Q40*) properties. It can help their wounds heal quickly. Some African clawed frogs can live up to 15 years in the wild and up to 30 years in captivity...

Test 3

Part 1

MAN:　　Good morning. This is the Children's Play Park. What can I do for you?

WOMAN:　Hi, this is Josephine speaking. I was just thinking about what to do on weekends, and then found your advertisement on the internet. The pictures on the ads are really attractive.

MAN:　　Thanks. We provide a friendly, safe and clean place for your children to have fun. Your kids will definitely have a pleasant experience here.

WOMAN:　That's nice. But my children are young, only about three years old. I don't know if it is suitable for them to play here.

MAN:　　That shouldn't be a problem. Our equipment is designed for children aged 6 months to 11 years (**Q1**). 3-year-old children can certainly find suitable play equipment here.

WOMAN:　OK, good. So what about the price?

MAN:　　It depends on the age of your kids. For those who are about 6 months old, it's one pound per hour. The older the kids are, the higher the price will be. But the maximum price is £3.85.

WOMAN:　Uh huh. Do I need to make reservations two or three days in advance? I'm afraid that there will be no room left.

MAN:　　It covers a large area. Most of the time the space is enough, so you don't have to book (**Q2**) in advance. Just come here directly.

WOMAN:　OK, that sounds good. Are there any facilities for kids to explore new activities?

MAN:　　Sure. We have many different entertainment areas and some are only open to babies (**Q3**). These areas are filled with cushions, so they can have fun on them. And cushions are also used to protect them from getting injured. You can rest assured that children's safety will be of paramount importance.

WOMAN:　Well, that's thoughtful. I'm curious about what else is in the play park?

MAN:　　We have built many entertainment devices to improve children's fitness, such as slides, which are one of children's favorite things to play with. Also, there are some bridges (**Q4**) and tunnels, which train their sense of balance.

WOMAN:　Sounds interesting. Is there a place where kids can play ball games? Like basketball, for example.

MAN:　　We certainly do. Actually, it's a pitch where they can play all kinds of ball games, including basketball. If there are more than five kids, we will also help to organize football (**Q5**) and volleyball matches.

WOMAN: My kids would love that!

....

WOMAN: Oh, do you have any classes?

MAN: Yes. What kind of classes are you looking for?

WOMAN: My daughter has indulged in singing these days. I wonder if it's possible for her to join a music class?

MAN: I'm so sorry. We haven't had any music classes yet. But we do have dancing classes. And another course, drama (**Q6**), is also well-liked by almost all kids. You can ask your daughter if she is interested in it.

WOMAN: Alright. How about parties? Will there be any parties?

MAN: Absolutely. We have different theme parties every week. In these parties, children are encouraged to perform in public to show their talents. The party host will also arrange some games (**Q7**) for the children to improve their sense of cooperation.

WOMAN: What's the theme of the party this week?

MAN: Because they have distinct interests and hobbies, we will organize parties for girls and boys separately. For girls, they can pose with fun props like a lion tamer's flaming hoop.

WOMAN: Flaming hoop...That sounds like a circus (**Q8**) party, isn't it?

MAN: Yes. We will also serve some dessert for free, such as clown cupcakes.

WOMAN: What about boys?

MAN: Boys will enjoy a pirate party. Before the party, everyone will receive a telescope and a hat (**Q9**), so that they can play the part of pirates and immerse themselves in the party.

WOMAN: Perfect. Well, I would like to get a membership card for my children here. Who should I contact?

MAN: I will help you sign up for membership. Could you tell me your phone number? Oh, and we will assign you a private customer service staff. If you have any problems, don't hesitate to contact him. His telephone number is 016 1962 3388 (**Q10**).

WOMAN: Thank you.

Part 2

Hi guys! Welcome to the Melville Channel. I'm Beatrice. Today we're going to read some letters from our audience who plan to travel to Melville, this beautiful island or who have already been here before, and I'll answer any questions they might have. I believe the issues they mention will be useful to you if you also want to visit this place. Now let's begin, shall we?

The first letter is from Jenny. She's curious about giving tips for taxi drivers and guides. Let's see... Oh, Jenny says actually she's been to Melville once before and she even got her hair done on the island. Haha, really? I wonder how was it. Well, Jenny says she was quite satisfied with the service but she didn't know how much she should've tipped her hairdresser. Anyway, she ended up giving him 10% of the total bill. Right, when you're in a restaurant or hair salon here, usually the tip is about 10%. But for taxi drivers or guides, you're free to tip any amount you want. (*Q11*) There isn't any rule on this, although the guides may expect you to give a lot.

Jenny is also asking about what one should do if she needs a doctor. Well, firstly, you need to know that there will be a charge (*Q12*). There are English-speaking doctors in the clinics and hospitals on the island to take care of visitors from around the world, but you have to pay the medical bills yourself. Normally, the medical services can be really pricey, so you'd better buy some medical insurance before coming here. It'll be too late to call the insurance company after you get hurt or sick. Oh, and don't call the hotel doctor. They are not very helpful and are usually slow to respond.

That's pretty much it for Jenny's letter. Now let's hear what Alice has to say. Okay, so, Alice has also travelled to the island before and she wants to share her experience with us. She mentions one thing particular—the drinking water on the island. Alright, I know where she's going. Firstly, of course the tap water is safe to drink, so you don't have to worry at all. It's just that there are some minerals in it, so it may taste a bit strange to some people, like our Alice (*Q13*). It's not harmful. You'll get used to it, or you can choose to buy bottled water instead. Alice says you can find it in almost every corner of the island and the price is not high, so it's really convenient (*Q14*). But she also reminds us that sometimes people might simply put the tap water into a bottle for sale. So guys, remember to check if the lid has already been opened before you buy it.

She also talks about the buses. Well, there are not many buses on the island but they are all very reliable, because they stick to a fixed schedule and always arrive on time (*Q15*). But you should be prepared for the bumpy roads here. The journey might not be as smooth as you imagine. What's more, be aware that not all buses show their numbers in the front. Sometimes it might just show the destination instead, but that can also be wrong. And finally, the bus might not pull over at some stops. So, if you want to know where a bus is heading and where it will stop along the way, it's best that you go and ask the driver directly (**Q16**).

Okay, now let's check out our third letter. It's from Daniel. Hmmm... He wants to find some information about the car renting services here. Sure thing. If you fancy a self-driving tour around the island, you can always rent a car, but don't just call a rental company and hope that they will take care of everything. Most of the time you can't get through to them at all and some companies may overcharge you. Don't turn to the hotel receptionist either. It's possible that the hotel is working with the companies to fleece the tourists for a commission. Here's what you should do. Find out the prices of different companies and then choose the best option among them (**Q17**).

Despite the occasionally unreasonable prices, normally the companies are lawful businesses and have all the certificates required for operation, so you don't have to worry about the after-sale service. But when you go to fetch the car, make sure they clarify with you about all the content of the services you've bought with them (**Q18**). For example, some packages provide unlimited mileage and some come with free maps. Sometimes there might be seasonal promotions but you'll have to cancel your booked service if you want to participate in them. That's what you need to know about car-renting. I hope that helps.

Alright, let's move on to the next letter from Tom. Tom's also concerned about transportation. But instead of renting a car, he prefers getting a taxi, so he's wondering if it will be hard to find one on the road here and he'd like to learn about the pricing. Well, first of all, availability won't be a problem because there are enough taxis in most places. So, if you want one, you don't have to reserve it online or call a taxi rank. They'll just arrange a nearby one for you anyway. Just go and flag down the one passing by you. It's the quickest way (**Q19**). As for how much they will charge you, probably many people would agree that the fairest way is to charge according to distance, so they'd turn on the meter after you get in the car. But the thing is, some taxis here don't have a meter and some people are even required to pay extra money when they arrive at the destination, especially at night. Considering that, my advice is, you should ask the driver how much the ride is gonna cost and reach an agreement with him right at the beginning (**Q20**). That way, you won't have any dispute over the price...

Now let's hear what others have to say...

Part 3

MAN:	Hi, Sue. Sorry I'm late.
WOMAN:	That's OK, but we really do need to get started on planning this seminar presentation. We've only got a week before we present it to the rest of the class. Are you still happy with the original topic?
MAN:	You mean aircraft engine design?
WOMAN:	Yes.
MAN:	It's fine with me. I'm afraid I haven't had a chance to finish the reading yet. But I have been thinking about the structure of the presentation. And I thought we could begin by looking at the problems associated with current aircraft engines.
WOMAN:	Sounds reasonable.
MAN:	We could get the other students to suggest the problems. What do you think?
WOMAN:	It might be better to ask questions. Otherwise, they may not suggest all the relevant ones (**Q21**).
MAN:	You're right.
WOMAN:	Then there has to be some direct input from us.
MAN:	Hm, but we should keep the lecture part brief (**Q22**), and then do something different to stop people falling asleep.
WOMAN:	What?
MAN:	Oh, umm, maybe an activity they have to do in threes or fours toward the end of the seminar?
WOMAN:	Yes, they could discuss the alternatives.
MAN:	Or, even better, why not get the groups to actually draw the engine designs?
WOMAN:	Great idea. Discussions can be a bit boring.
MAN:	Hm. What else do we need to do?
WOMAN:	Well, we also have to think about what we need to help us to get the main ideas across.
MAN:	How do you mean?
WOMAN:	Well, will we have all of the information on slides, say?(**Q23**)
MAN:	Okay.

MAN:	So we'd better start jotting down the order we're going to present the information. Got any paper?
WOMAN:	Yes, hang on. Now let's think. Well, first we need to establish what's wrong with the way things are at the moment, with regard to aircraft engine design.
MAN:	Hm.

WOMAN: And we should bring the focus specifically onto the environmental issues (**Q24**).

MAN: Yes, because that's really the whole purpose of looking at the new designs.

WOMAN: So, after that, why don't we talk about the future situation? We need to stress that even when petrol production begins to slow down in a few years (**Q25**), it won't be the end of our problems, because there are alternatives like tar sands and, um, what's the other stuff?

MAN: Oil shale?

WOMAN: Right, oil shale.

MAN: And we really don't ever need to worry about either of those in terms of supply (**Q26**). There are huge amounts available. Using them would mean that we could just go on using the same engines as we are now, and producing just as much pollution.

WOMAN: Exactly. So CO_2 levels won't change.

MAN: Right.

WOMAN: So then we need to put forward the safer alternative energy sources.

MAN: And these need to be related to the two designs we're going to present later on.

WOMAN: Yes, so there's the idea of using batteries instead of fuel-based engines (**Q27**).

MAN: Yes, and there's hydrogen fuels.

WOMAN: Right. What else do we need to add?

MAN: Umm... the next thing is probably to look at the problems we think will be identified with those alternatives.

WOMAN: Yes. People are always worried about changing to totally new forms of technology. Well, I suppose that the first protest will be how expensive they are (**Q28**).

MAN: That's number one. We don't need to spend too much time on that because it's not too hard to understand.

WOMAN: Hm.

MAN: What other problems are there?

WOMAN: Uh...I guess I'd have to say the next difficulty would be how to generate and store the power from those sources (**Q29**).

MAN: Sure. No one's really come up with a way to do that effectively or cheaply yet.

WOMAN: And of course, finally...

MAN: Our topic...

MAN & WOMAN (TOGETHER): Engine design! (LAUGHING)

MAN: Because current engines are only designed to run on petroleum-based fuels (**Q30**).

WOMAN: Perfect. This is going to be good.

MAN: Sure hope so.

Part 4

For my presentation today, I've chosen an American photographer called Andreas Feininger. I found a few of his books in the library, and there are several websites if you would like to find out some more information on him. Andreas Feininger spent most of his working life in the United States, and he died there in 1999. But he was born in Germany. His career was unusual, because he trained as an architect before becoming a photographer.

I decided I wanted to learn more about him when I recently saw his photographs of New York. Some of them are really familiar, because you see them a lot on posters (*Q31*). I didn't realize that they had all been taken by the same photographer. Feininger worked as an architect in offices in Germany and France. But he decided to pursue photography as a career and moved to New York. He worked for *Life* magazine for 20 years and completed more than 430 assignments. He particularly liked to photograph wide views of cities and different lights. But what really made him stand out from other photographers was his fascination with the idea of photographing— not just the beauty of cities, but showing them as a living, dynamic organism, sometimes even violent, with all their confusion and even their ugliness (*Q32*). Although he loved his work for *Life* magazine and had many opportunities to travel, he left in 1962 because he was eager to produce books of his photographs and techniques (*Q33*). However, he continued to take photos of urban scenes, many of which are regarded as classic works today.

During Feininger's life, he had many exhibitions and published many books. The first major photographic exhibition to include his work took place in 1955 at the Museum of Modern Art, when Feininger was one of the several photographers represented in an exhibition (*Q34*) called The Family of Man. Two years later, in 1957, he had a solo exhibition of his nature themed works (*Q35*), which, for the first time, were mainly taken in color. He continued having exhibitions after he left *Life* magazine. The largest of these was in 1977, which was a retrospective exhibition of the International Center of Photography, bringing together photos taken at different stages of his life (*Q36*). There are permanent collections of his works in a number of galleries and museums in the states in Germany.

Now, as for the books, Feininger has published a lot, but they're not all available. I've got a few here. The first one is called *New York in the Forties*, so that tells you what it's about. Most of the photos are of buildings in the city, and they clearly show the methods (*Q37*) he was so well known for. The second one's title is *America Yesterday*. It covers the 1940s to 1960s, and most of the photos are urban. Unlike some of his other books though, the photos aren't just of the center of American cities, but the suburbs too and their industries. It includes the famous 1942 Midtown Manhattan shot, taken from 25 miles away. In fact, all of the subjects in this book were photographed outdoors (*Q38*), and there are some wonderful ideas in this book that can help us improve our own photographs. For example, Feininger always shows great understanding of the importance of light (*Q39*), and that's clearly displayed in this collection of photos. The third book, *That's Photography*, is a collection of photographs of different places and eras, and contains many of his most famous ones. But it has a couple of essays (*Q40*) which gave me a fascinating insight into his approach to photography.

Well, I think Andreas Feininger was a really fantastic photographer, and if you go and look at these books, you'll see why.

Test 4

Part 1

Father: Hey, Nancy. The holiday is coming but I'll be away for a whole week, so we may need to come up with a plan for Lily. I already have some ideas in mind but you're welcome to offer your advice.

Nanny: Sure!

Father: So, we need to think about what you're gonna do each day, from Monday to Friday.

Nanny: No problem. What do you have in mind, then?

Father: Well, on Monday, I'm thinking that perhaps you can take Lily to watch a film. Lily is enthusiastic about adventure movies.

Nanny: She'd love that.

Father: I happen to have two 10-pound coupons for you. You'll spend just 20 pounds on two tickets with these coupons.

Nanny: Oh no, no, no, actually a ticket won't cost 10 pounds at all. During the holiday, it only sells at a price of £9.15. And if you book online in advance, it's even cheaper. You only need to pay £8.25 (**Q1**) for each ticket.

Father: Wow, I didn't know that. Right, remember to bring something to drink for Lily, because the film may last for a long time. But don't bring anything with sugar in it, like juice.

Nanny: Yeah, sugar might be bad for her teeth. Why not bring her some water?

Father: Water (**Q2**) is great! Alright, then it's settled. What about Tuesday?

Nanny: Umm, why don't we have some outdoor activities on Tuesday?

Father: Great idea! I know our community has organised a walk (**Q3**) for families on that day, so you can go out for a walk together and get some fresh air.

Nanny: Sure! Where is it gonna take place?

Father: They used to carry out the activity in the Central Square, but now they've moved to the woods (**Q4**). Remember, the activity begins at 10:15 a.m., so don't be late.

Nanny: I see. We'd better get there at 10:00 a.m.(**Q5**), so we'll have to leave at 9:00 just in case.

Father: Right, another thing. There have been frequent showers recently, so the paths could be muddy that day. You might need to take Lily's boots (**Q6**) with you.

Nanny: I'll keep that in mind.

Father: Okay, now let's talk about what to do on Wednesday. Oh, her cousin (**Q7**) has invited her to his party that day. I'm sure the kids will have a good time together.

Nanny: That's great. Where will the party be held?

Father: The original plan was to have the party at the amusement park, but in the end they changed the location to High Street. There is a Japanese restaurant (**Q8**) that the kids really love.

Nanny: Alright, I'll drive her there. As for Thursday, I checked the calendar and Lily has music lessons on that day every week. Is she still having the class during the holiday?

Father: Oh, yes, yes. I almost forgot about that. The lesson should go on as planned. Take her to Huskey Hall. The lesson starts at 2 o'clock in the afternoon. And you have to pay (**Q9**) for the fees at the end of each lesson. Make sure you've got enough money with you.

Nanny: No worries. I'll write it down in my notebook right now.

Father: Wow, you are so organized. What about the last day? Any ideas?

Nanny: Mm... How about storytelling? My friend's kid loves that and I think Lily will be interested in it too.

Father: Good idea!

Nanny: It's held at that bookstore in the city centre.

Father: Oh! Actually, we have been there before. It's a nice and tidy place. I really like it! Oh, the laundry should be ready by then. Could you please go and pick up the clothes on your way back?

Nanny: Sure.

Father: And I remember there is a post office near the laundry. It'd be really nice of you if you could also buy some stamps (**Q10**) for me. We're running out of them at home.

Nanny: No problem. It sounds like it'll be a really fun week...

Part 2

WOMAN:　Hello, Mr. Johnson. It is a great honour to have you here with us to shed some light on the environmental issues in Auckland. We all care about our city and would love to know what has been done to ensure its sustainable development.

MAN:　Thank you. I understand that our environment has become a public concern in recent years. I will begin by introducing the current status, then, in particular, the water quality situation.

WOMAN:　Sure!

MAN:　In the city of Auckland, there are mainly two types of water environment. The first one is fresh water, such as streams in mountains or lakes in parks. They provide the necessary environment for a wide variety of plants and animals to flourish, and few issues have been reported concerning water quality. The sea water, on the contrary, suffers from having a substantially lower quality due to human activities (*Q11*). You can see lots of bottles and plastic bags thrown around on beaches, which may later be swept into the sea, together with industrial waste water from the urban areas, causing pollution to the marine environment. But the government has already enacted some policies to address the problem and some conservation societies are also making efforts to raise people's awareness in this regard.

WOMAN:　Well, at least we know people are doing something to arrest the decline of water quality. Are there any other conservation projects in Auckland?

MAN:　Sure, there are a lot, but there is one in particular I want to talk about. That is Project Tiri, short for Tiritiri Matangi, which is an island rich in Māori and European history with one of the most successful community-led conservation projects in the world.

MAN:　Just forty years ago, Tiritiri Matangi, located near Auckland in the Hauraki Gulf Marine Park, was almost completely bare of forest following 120 years of farming. Between 1984 and 1994, thousands of volunteers, following previous practices of similar projects, planted more than 250,000 trees and plants, with seeds sourced from Tiritiri Matangi and nearby islands as well to boost plant biodiversity. The unique vision of this project was to build an 'open sanctuary' for wildlife, which placed people at the heart of the project by allowing the public to be involved in the creation and evolution of this sanctuary (*Q12*).

MAN:　The ecological restoration of Tiritiri Matangi has always been underpinned by firm ecological science. There is a permanent scientific research centre based on the island, so you can probably get a view of what the volunteers will be doing here: instead of revegetation like in the past, now they will get a chance to be involved in real research studies in the field, including species conservation, biodiversity monitoring, and invasive species management, furthering their science skills (*Q13*).

The island is open for tours if the tourists would like to get a closer look of the life there.

MAN: The programme has proved to be very rewarding for the volunteers according to their previous testimonials. Apart from being a plus while applying for universities, the biggest bonus of this volunteering experience is that they get to be a part of a wonderful team of excellent people from around the world. They will learn how to cooperate and strive for the same goal (**Q14**). Some even say the field work has also enabled them to lose a few pounds!

WOMAN: It certainly sounds very tempting. I believe many of our audience are already wondering what we should take with us if we're to sign up for the volunteering work.

MAN: Well, there are all the equipment you might need on the island, so you don't have to worry about that. And the tap water is drinkable there, so no need to bring anything to drink either. You may need to bring some food in case you get hungry during the work (**Q15**).

....

WOMAN: So, it seems there are quite a lot of conservation projects in New Zealand. Could you recommend some activities the volunteers can do in other popular ones, Mr. Johnson?

MAN: Absolutely. Well, volunteers can contribute in a number of ways. For example, on the Great Mercury Island, you will help with the bioresearch and monitoring work. Besides using some special underwater equipment to observe the marine creatures and plants, you can also get into the water to have a closer look at the mysterious ocean yourself (**Q16**). There will be professional divers going down there regularly to collect some samples for analysis and also retrieve the rubbish along the way, so you won't have to pick them up.

MAN: Then there is the Treasure Island project, in which you can participate in the heritage restoration. You will be given a tour around the ancient buildings and even help with their renovation (**Q17**). I'm sure it will be both a fun and meaningful experience.

MAN: The Coal Island is a very popular destination, too. Surrounded by mountains, it's a successful natural reserve home to many rare species. Here you can take a hike deep into the mountains and get in touch with nature (**Q18**).

MAN: Oh, I also recommend the Waikite Valley. The Department of Conservation has committed a lot of resources into restoring vulnerable species in the valley after grazing animals significantly damaged the area. So, as a volunteer, you can take part in the huge revegetation movement (**Q19**).

MAN: Tuatapera Hump Ridge is another interesting place to go. The project seeks to build the place into a stunning addition to the Great Walks network. Located in the south-west corner of the South Island, the Tuatapere Hump Ridge Track journeys through spectacular and diverse landscapes, including seascapes, sandy beaches, native forests and an alpine environment with soaring limestone tors. Though the Track has been open for 20 years, a lot of upgrade work is required to ensure its long-term access to the public. Sign up to be a volunteer, and you can get the opportunity to have hands-on experience of track construction and repair (*Q20*).

WOMAN: That sounds like lots of fun...

Part 3

TUTOR:	Hi, Brian. What's the matter?
STUDENT:	Hi Professor, I'm here to ask for some advice on my paper on bilingual learning of babies.
TUTOR:	Alright. Did you have problems finding information about this topic?
STUDENT:	Actually, I've already read lots of materials online. There are many studies on this topic, so it's not hard to gather the information I need.
TUTOR:	That's good. What's the problem, then?
STUDENT:	Well, I've narrowed down my research to one specific area, but I'm currently struggling over how to put my thoughts together into a well-organized paper (*Q21*).
TUTOR:	I see. So, could you tell me why you decided to study this topic in the first place?
STUDENT:	Well, researchers used to believe that a bilingual environment had some downsides to children's development, so at first I was also put off by this topic.
TUTOR:	Really? Then why did you change your mind? Is it because few students have chosen the same topic?
STUDENT:	It's true that not many have, but it doesn't influence me. Actually, this area aroused my interest when I discovered that critics had changed their tune regarding bilingualism (*Q22*) as time went by. So, I wanted to investigate what effects it will really have on children.
TUTOR:	Interesting. Have you researched into how people's opinions have changed over time? Why did they think poorly of bilingual education in the past?
STUDENT:	Yes. When it comes to bilingual education, our first reaction is probably that children's proficiency in either of the languages will never match up with the level of monolingual native speakers. However, that was not the real reason why people were sceptical of bilingual education in the past.
TUTOR:	So what was it then?
STUDENT:	The truth was, back then, it was commonly believed that learning two languages simultaneously could easily confuse children (*Q23*). For instance, a child born into a family with his father speaking English and his mother speaking Italian may sometimes speak in English but use Italian grammar by mistake.
TUTOR:	That's true. Actually, recent evidence also reveals that bilingual children might not be able to start speaking either of their languages when other monolingual kids have already begun.
STUDENT:	Right. I've also read similar research on bilingual children's speech delay, but actually it just takes them a bit longer to become fluent in both languages, and people have come to realise the benefits of bilingualism for children. Nowadays, many people are even trying to create a bilingual environment for their kids because they assume that

mastering several languages will help them get a better job when they grow up.

TUTOR:　Yeah...but that's only what those anxious parents are concerned about and is not necessarily the case. Are there any other benefits?

STUDENT:　Well, researchers found that children who knew two languages performed better on attention tests and had better concentration compared to those who spoke only one language. So it seems that it's easier for them to do well academically.

TUTOR:　That makes sense, but that's still not the most essential skill a kid can gain from a bilingual learning environment.

STUDENT:　Mm... You're right. Since the child has to cope with two different languages at a time, it's been proven that their multi-tasking ability will be stronger than others' (**Q24**).

TUTOR:　That's it. Since bilingual children have to constantly switch between two languages, their brains apparently are wired to toggle back and forth between different tasks depending on the circumstances.

STUDENT:　Right, due to these advantages, many parents are now making efforts to cultivate their kids' bilingual ability. To meet the market's demand, there are also lots of bilingual learning institutes out there. But the biggest problem is it can be rather costly for parents (**Q25**).

TUTOR:　Exactly. To create an ideal environment, parents also like to take their kids to some extracurricular bilingual activities, like multi-language clubs with children from similar backgrounds.

STUDENT:　That's right...

TUTOR:　So how's your literature review going?

STUDENT:　I've already read a wide range of research in this field. Richard Floridi was one of the pioneers who realised the significance of bilingualism on children's development, so he tracked the lives of some bilingual children to find out its long-term effects on them.

TUTOR:　Definitely. His work was ground-breaking but due to limited conditions at that time, he couldn't gather enough volunteers so there were not enough samples (**Q26**) to support his conclusions.

STUDENT:　Yes, that's a real pity, but his work has inspired many later researchers. For example, Professor Woodcock, from the University of Southampton, enlarged the sample size and furthered his studies.

TUTOR:　Right, although he'd got enough data, the sources of it were not very reliable. Instead of participating in the investigation himself, he just collected those bilingual children's cases from different places and he failed to carry out an in-depth analysis of the materials (**Q27**).

STUDENT: I see... I also read Professor Granger's research. She's one of the leading neuroscientists exploring how the brains of bilingual kids work.

TUTOR: Yes, her team conducted lots of experiments, like comparing the different brain structures of bilingual kids and monolingual kids, and observing how bilingual environments change the children's brains in the long term.

STUDENT: That's right. And she explained all her experiments in an elaborate way, including her hypothesis, methods, data collection, analysis and so on (**Q28**).

TUTOR: Absolutely. There are lots of profound insights in her studies for you to dig into.

STUDENT: Sure. I'll bear that in mind.

TUTOR: Also, there is a professor named Brito whose work is on your must-read list.

STUDENT: Oh really? What's special about his studies?

TUTOR: He recorded the daily conversations of normal bilingual families and observed how the babies gradually built their vocabulary, mastered grammar and switched between different languages, and he did this using cutting-edge speech analysis equipment in his laboratory (**Q29**).

STUDENT: That sounds cool.

TUTOR: Oh right, and the studies of Maria Baralt are also worth reading. Her research interest is how the growth of globalisation has motivated bilingual education in society (**Q30**), and she mainly focuses on America, a typical immigrant country.

STUDENT: Okay, I'll go and find out more about her...

Part 4

Good morning, everyone. Welcome to today's lecture about the development plan for Barningham. In the past few years, great changes have taken place there, and today, Barningham is at a turning point. Opportunities are emerging to transform perceptions of the town, addressing its negative image and setting high standards for the future.

Barningham, which is about 116 kilometres north-east of London, has long been recognized as an area of strategic importance with the potential to become a more people-friendly town and a flourishing commercial center. Situated in the countryside of England, it currently has a population of about 16,000, all of whom are hard-working people shining in all walks of life.

Decades ago, most citizens built up their fortune through the furniture (*Q31*) business, which was the town's most well-known industry in the past. The sofas, wardrobes and tables they made were very popular in nearby cities because of their high degree of craftsmanship, and were exported in large quantities every year, accounting for half of the local GDP. However, recent years have witnessed some transformations in the town's various industries. As time has gone by, the service (*Q32*) sector has gradually risen to become the most important industry in this town, making up 2/3 of all the industries. For example, financial services have been booming these years, and one big insurance (*Q33*) company has hired 600 workers since its establishment.

Also, Barningham is one of the most accessible places by road. As a town near London, it has bad traffic. So, emphasis should be given to tackling congestion in these areas, especially near the schools (*Q34*) in the centre of the town. As parents usually pick up their children there, it leads to problems in nearby traffic. Another thing to be noted is that the frequency of railways is a bit low, so it fails to meet the basic needs of local residents, let alone tourists.

In order to make Barningham a better living place, there are measures in place to improve its competitiveness within the next five years. To begin with, the town is campaigning to bring in more talents. So, first of all, it will enlarge its residential area by establishing 16,000 new houses, providing enough room for newcomers to settle in. What's more, more employment opportunities will be created to ensure the livelihood of the increasing population and to stimulate the economy. An estimate of 20,000 new jobs (*Q35*) will be provided to the local residents. Scientific research is another key area of Barningham's development plan. The local university aims to establish a scientific and technological incubator to enhance its research ability, which will be supported and co-funded by the government. The university also plans to set up a new campus (*Q36*) nearby to build more laboratories.

Transport and accessibility play an essential role in urban development. Therefore, there are also some policies targeted at reducing the road congestion and improving the town's connectivity with the surrounding cities. The local government is making efforts to mitigate traffic (*Q37*) flow by 20% through its five-year plan. For this purpose, private cars are discouraged on the roads. Instead, cycling (*Q38*), as an eco-friendly mode of transport, is strongly advocated, so you can expect to see more new cycle routes across the city in the following years! Apart from that, more railways will be built and more trains will be provided to create an efficient transport network around the area.

The next phase of the plan identifies some specific development areas to meet the demand for the booming businesses. Increased investment from the government will allow the town to allocate 10,000 square metres to establish supermarkets, shopping malls and department stores, promoting the vitality of retail (*Q39*) businesses. Besides that, about 8,000 square metres have been designated for the construction of office (*Q40*) areas, so more skyscrapers will rise up in the central business district in the near future.

The town is also aiming to become a popular tourist destination, so it's working on the renovation of several landmarks...

Test 5

Part 1

MAN: Hello, this is Community College. How can I help you?

WOMAN: Hi. I saw some advertisements online about the classes you offer and I'm calling to find out more about them.

MAN: Sure. We provide a wide range of courses here. May I ask what you are particularly interested in?

WOMAN: I'm thinking about learning a musical instrument, maybe guitar. I see that there is a guitar class here, right?

MAN: That's right. It's open every Thursday and the fee is 80 dollars for 6 classes. That's a pretty good price.

WOMAN: Sounds great! When does the class usually begin?

MAN: Well, we have two separate schedules for different levels of students. If you've never learned guitar before, the class begins at 7:45 (*Q1*) in the morning, while for those who already have some basic knowledge, it starts earlier at 7:00 a.m.

WOMAN: Alright. Should I bring my own guitar to the class then?

MAN: Yes, you should. And you'd better bring something you can write (*Q2*) on to take notes during the class, like some pieces of paper. There can be a lot to take in, especially for someone who's totally new at it.

WOMAN: You're right. I won't forget that. I also want to acquire some knowledge of first aid. I think that can be very important, especially when there's any emergency. Could you tell me more about this course?

MAN: Absolutely! It's on Tuesday every week and it costs 140 (*Q3*) dollars for 4 classes in total. It used to be 120 dollars but we had to raise the price to cover the cost.

WOMAN: That's alright. I totally understand.

MAN: Oh, and if you want to learn more first aid skills and knowledge, there's also an advanced course after you finish this one. And if you can pass all the tests in it, you'll receive a qualification.

WOMAN: Terrific! Is there anything I need to bring to the class?

MAN: No, you don't need to bring anything. We provide all the tools needed here.

WOMAN: Great. That's very convenient. What about the Asian Cooking class on Wednesday? Actually, I've taken this course 2 years ago and I liked it very much. Now I feel like taking it again and I just want to see if everything is still the same. I remember the fee was 60 dollars back then. Is it still the same now?

MAN: Well, yes, the course fee is still 60 dollars but you will also still need to pay an additional 56 (*Q4*) dollars for the ingredients you will use during the class. So, 60 dollars plus 56 dollars, that's 116 dollars in total.

WOMAN: Okay.

MAN: At the beginning of the course, every student will be given a manual for free, and after you finish all the classes, you'll receive a certificate (*Q5*).

WOMAN: I can't wait to begin. Oh, I remember we have to bring a knife to the cooking class, right? (*Q6*)

MAN: That's right. You also need to bring some bowls or plates for the seasonings or other ingredients.

WOMAN: No problem.

....

WOMAN: You know what? My daughter is also interested in some of the classes here. She's looking for some slow exercises.

MAN: Then I recommend Tai-Chi! It's very relaxing and is gaining increasing popularity among young people. The price is only 70 dollars. I think your daughter would like it.

WOMAN: That's a good choice. Is everyone wearing a Tai-Chi uniform in class?

MAN: No, there isn't a specific dress code. Just wear something comfortable and loose.

WOMAN: Okay. I will let her know.

MAN: She can also consider taking the yoga class, which especially suits women. It's on Thursday and the cost is also 70 dollars.

WOMAN: Right! I think some yoga moves would be good for her neck(*Q7*). She's a college student and uses the computer a lot, so she's been suffering from neck pain from time to time.

MAN: I see. It would certainly help.

WOMAN: Does she need to wear any special footwear for the class?

MAN: No need at all. During the class, everyone does yoga on the floor so you don't even have to wear any shoes.

WOMAN: Alright. She will just bring a towel (*Q8*) then. She might also need a mat, but I suppose that's provided in the class?

MAN: Yes. There is a special mat for all the students.

WOMAN: Perfect. And my niece hopes to learn how to do makeup. I heard that you have courses here for that, is it true?

MAN: Yes. You can choose to take the class on Monday evening or Saturday afternoon. The course fee is only 38 dollars.

WOMAN: Great. I guess Saturday will be better.

MAN: Okay. We teach both day and night makeup and the class will be held in Lawnton Community Centre.

WOMAN: Lawnton? Could you spell it out for me?

MAN: L-A-W-N-T-O-N (**Q9**).

WOMAN: Okay. Should she bring her own makeup or is it provided?

MAN: Oh, all students should use their own makeup. Also, don't forget to ask her to bring some brushes and a small mirror (**Q10**).

WOMAN: Of course. I'll make sure she brings everything.

Part 2

WOMAN: Alright everyone, today we have a special guest with us. Let's welcome... Jim! Jim has recently participated in a volunteer activity which includes living for six months in a British village that replicates life during the Iron Age. And now he's going to tell us how he felt about the everyday life there. So Jim, could you describe to us what a normal day was like in such an ancient village?

MAN: Hi, guys. Well, I'd say the biggest difference is that I've come to get up really early every morning (**Q11**). Before living in the village, I always liked to lie in even when I had already woken up, so that I could enjoy the "me time" for a while. But in the village, everyone got up so early—you could hear them washing up and starting their day at 5 or 6 in the morning. Some of them complained that it was because they couldn't sleep well due to the coldness at night, though that was not really a problem for me. Gradually, I just went along with everyone and started waking up early too.

WOMAN: Early to bed and early to rise. That's a good habit, actually.

MAN: That's true. After we got up, we would start making breakfast. Usually we had porridge and fruits. It might put some people off when they hear that, but in fact it tasted good and was healthy too. We usually started preparing the ingredients the night before and spent much effort cooking it in the morning (**Q12**). We got used to it and started liking it in no time. And we would all just gather around and slowly enjoy the meal.

WOMAN: That sounds nice. What about your dinner?

MAN: Well, normally dinner was supposed to be an occasion for people to gather around and share their day, but in the village, sometimes we were too exhausted after a whole day's work. So, we'd just skip the meal and go to bed (**Q13**).

WOMAN: What did you usually have for dinner, then?

MAN: Most of the time we ate fruits, berries, nuts and all sorts of things we gathered in the woods.

WOMAN: Wow, did everyone need to go out and collect food?

MAN: Yes, all of us participated in the food gathering task, but there was still a division of labour in this small community. Everyone took on several jobs at a time but each had a different priority. For example, for a blacksmith, his main job was to make sure that the fire in the house kept burning so that people wouldn't suffer from coldness (**Q14**). It allowed people to carry out all the other tasks. Besides that, the blacksmith was also responsible for repairing the broken tools and other equipment.

WOMAN: It seems everyone was living a busy and fulfilling life there. What would you say was the favourite part of your whole experience there, Jim?

MAN: You know what, what I especially loved about the life there was everybody had many different things to do (**Q15**). We would never get bored. And we also gained some new knowledge from all sorts of activities. Another unexpected bonus was I even lost some weight at the end of the program. I guess it was due to all the physical work every day.

In the village, we all lived in a particular kind of house—the wooden roundhouse, which was the most prominent type of housing built in Britain from the Bronze Age all the way up to the Iron Age. We built the houses on our own by hand, using the natural materials available to us from the land. Now let me describe the basic procedures you need to follow to build a wooden roundhouse, because it's quite interesting.

First of all, you need to determine the location where you want to build the roundhouse. You decide the centre point and use the pegs to mark it out (**Q16**). And then you should move on to its perimeter. Draw a circle as large as you would like the house to be, and point out where you want to plant the posts, which will later serve as the main structure of the house and support the roof.

So, in order to do that, next you need to dig in your marks and make some room for the posts. You will use some special hand-made tools, which come from animal bones (**Q17**). After that, you can fix those wooden posts, usually made of hazel branches, into the holes (**Q18**). When you finish setting up the surrounding posts, you can go on to put up a stake in the centre point.

Now, you can start building the walls, which is a ring of support poles weaved with wattling and plastered in daub. We've already set up the poles, so it's time to build the fences. Just weave those long, flexible sticks in and out of the upright posts. Hazel, which is pliable and grows naturally long, is a good species to use for wattle. Oak tree branches are also used in the process. Daubing is the method used to weather proof the wattle with a mixture of clay, sand, straw and manure.

With the walls of the roundhouse completed, you can climb up to the scaffold and start building the roof (**Q19**). The first thing you need to do is to raise the roof poles and bind them together with rope using more hazel rods. But before that, you should check that the roof poles are of equal length (**Q20**). Then, you bind a snake of reeds close to the foot of the roof to provide a stitching anchor for the thatch. And once you cover the roof with a thick layer of thatch, you're ready to move in your Iron Age roundhouse!

Part 3

TUTOR: Now, let me have a look at the progress of your research. Have you decided on the topic?

TOM: Yes. We are quite interested in re-branding and after going through many journals, we think this topic is worth exploring further.

TUTOR: Good. If you want to write about re-branding, I think you should explain branding first, and then switch the topic to re-branding.

SUE: Yeah, that's also what we thought. Regarding what branding is, we've read an article published by AMA, the American Marketing Association, and it said that "a brand is a name, term, design, symbol, or any other feature that identifies one seller's goods or services as distinct from those of other sellers".

TUTOR: Um, what do you think of this definition?

SUE: Well...it only mentioned products and services, but I think branding should include a wider range of aspects, such as product quality, culture, customers as well as marketing strategies, and so on (**Q21**).

TUTOR: I agree with you. Are you going to provide some specific examples of branding?

TOM: Yes. We've already made some notes of that. While we were looking for the importance of re-branding for enterprises, we found some cases of the failure of branding. For instance, a company called Debenhams, which was once famous for its clothes, eventually declared bankruptcy because of its failure in branding.

TUTOR: Oh, how exactly did it fail in its branding?

SUE: At first, they employed an internationally-renowned designer to redo their logo. Well, that's good I mean, because this new logo helped them gain a vast amount of investment and they went through a period of great prosperity. However, blinded by their temporary success, they thought they had no need to re-brand. So later on, when the commercial market changed rapidly, they fell behind in the competition (**Q22**).

TUTOR: That shows how important re-branding is for the survival of companies.

SUE: Oh, and I also read some books about project management.

TUTOR: Project management?

SUE: Yes. It's mainly about how to lead a team to achieve their goals within certain limitations, like time, budget, and scope.

TUTOR: Sounds interesting.

SUE: But what I am really concerned about is whether this practice can be applied to marketing (**Q23**). It's a pity that the book doesn't mention that.

TUTOR: There are some similarities between projects and marketing. I believe it can help, to some extent.

TOM: Speaking of project management, I also read a book called *Project Management* for the

Unofficial Project Manager. I strongly recommend it if you are interested in this topic.

SUE: Great. What's special about it?

TOM: Well, this book is continually being updated with lots of real-life examples. And the structure is pretty well-organized (**Q24**). I think, for those who are just getting started in the industry, it's easy to digest.

SUE: Thank you, Tom. I'll read it tonight. By the way, have you read the e-mail that I sent you yesterday?

TOM: The research about customers' comments on re-branding? I did. What impressed me most is that it uses a focus group.

SUE: Yes. Having a semi-structured interview is always conducive to bringing out customers' inner thoughts.

TOM: At the beginning, it introduces the history of the company, and then it provides many details about how the people in the focus group were gathered, which gave me a lot of inspiration (**Q25**).

SUE: Right. Also, I think its layout can be regarded as a good sample which we can definitely learn from.

TUTOR: Great. What kind of companies are you going to study?

SUE: We both have experience with large companies. But we didn't find enough papers about big companies to support our study. And you know, Lichfield is just a small town, and local companies are all pretty small. We believe that it's important to be able to gather data first-hand, so we decided to focus on smaller companies (**Q26**).

TUTOR: Good choice.

TUTOR: Have you added any cases about re-branding in your research?

SUE: Yes. Tom and I have investigated two different companies. What I have studied is an ice cream company named Pure Scoop. They spent a large amount of money on the reconstruction of their logo. They have even recruited an Italian designer to change the colour schemes to follow the newest trends. However, this logo does not match the old-fashioned style the company represents, which makes it lose its unique appeal (**Q27**).

TUTOR: That might be one reason for its failure. What else?

SUE: The money spent on the logo also caused the costs to go up 2% and a pro-rata increase in ice cream prices. According to customers, the increased prices are acceptable, but what they cannot accept is the change in the recipes (**Q28**). Most of their customers have not gotten used to the new flavour.

TUTOR: It seems that the company did not fully investigate the customers' preferences before their re-branding. What about you, Tom?

Test 5
录音文本

TOM: I studied a car wash company. They used brand-monitoring software to measure current brand perception and adjusted their price system. These measures helped them increase their brand's popularity for a while. However, they also tried to learn from their competitors, and when they applied the strategies to themselves, the results were disappointing. More specifically, when choosing a new site, they picked a place with few pedestrians and inconvenient transportation, leading to the shrinkage of their market share (**Q29**). Next, to differentiate itself from their competitors, the company began to target the luxury market. However, the economic situation here does not provide enough high-end customers for them to make ends meet (**Q30**).

TUTOR: Right. Before re-branding, you should ensure you have both solid reasoning and a plan for recovery as part of your post-rebrand strategy. Otherwise, you may face a lot of trouble. Now, I have some suggestions for you two. The first is ...(Faded)

Part 4

Good morning, I'm John Murray and I have been studying marine mammals and birds for the last few years. I'm really excited to share with you today a little about a different type of penguin--The African Penguin.

From the very name, it will be obvious to most of you that there are no African Penguins in the Antarctic. These particular penguins don't live where it's snowy and icy. Instead, they live in the southern hemisphere on offshore islands near the coast of southwestern Africa.

In common with all penguins, they have to adapt to weather conditions so as to maintain a constant body temperature(*Q31*). But unlike other penguins the African species needs to find ways of staying cool. One of the ways they do this is by confining their movement (*Q32*) into early evening and early morning. Also in order to protect themselves from the intense heat of the daytime sun, they establish their homes by making hollows or nests beneath the roots (*Q33*) of trees. This results in them spreading out more than regular penguins who stay very close together in groups to share each other's body heat. In addition, African penguins spend a lot of time swimming in the sea to keep cool. And they also use physiological responses such as panting to avoid any heat stress.

Possibly the most well-known fact is that all penguins, including African ones, can swim but can't fly. This is due to them having solid and very dense bones(*Q34*). Most birds have a more hollow skeletal structure and are lighter, which helps them to fly easily. However, the weight of the penguins can be a distinct advantage as it helps them to dive and catch fish. The average dive of an African penguin lasts about two and a half minutes. And though depths of up to 130 meters have been recorded, they typically go down to around 30 meters. When on the hunt for small fish such as herring and squid, they can reach a top speed of nearly 20 kilometers an hour. The distance they have to travel to find food on land though, varies considerably. A typical trip could range between 30 and 70 kilometers, but can sometimes cover 110 kilometers. An interesting factor related to their eating patterns is the annual moult. The entire period of shedding feathers (*Q35*) takes about 20 days to complete. Both five weeks before and after this yearly occurrence, the penguins need to fatten up as they have reduced their body weight by almost half.

Okay. Well, let's move on to consider some of the major threats to their survival. The African penguin was recently placed on the endangered species list. The present population is probably less than 10% of that in 1990. Over the last 50 years, their numbers have decreased by 80%, which is pretty astonishing. Initially, the reasons for this significant decline were due mostly to the exploitation of penguin eggs for food and other factors related to habitat change. However, this has changed with current factors being primarily overfishing by commercial boat and pollution

Test 5 录音文本

(*Q36*). Aside from these man-made causes, there is also fierce competition with seals for space (*Q37*) in which to live, and also for food. These penguins also face attacks from sharks (*Q38*), which pose a large problem. Another such predaceous sea mammal for them is the sea lion. Threats can also come from the air, with gulls preying on the penguin chicks(*Q39*).

Given the steady annual rate of decline in the African penguin population, preservation is hugely important. As such, marine scientists have begun to recommend which penguins should breed with other penguins. The aim is to be able to maintain a healthy diversity (*Q40*) genetically within the population across the continent over a very long period of time. It has also been recommended that a health assessment...

Test 6

Part 1

MAN: Hello, Melbourne Sports Camp, Allen speaking.

WOMAN: Oh, hello. I'm thinking about sending my son to a sports camp. Are you the right person to speak to?

MAN: Yes, I am. Our camp is full of fun activities and I believe you will find some classes that are suitable for him.

WOMAN: Right. What classes do you have then?

MAN: Well, we offer some classes for ball games, such as baseball classes and tennis classes. Basketball classes are likely to be introduced, but we need to double check the schedule with the coach. Also, you can join swimming (*Q1*) classes if your kid is interested in water sports.

WOMAN: That's great. When will the classes begin?

MAN: The classes start on the 1st of June and goes on till the 25th, and all the classes will be held at High (*Q2*) Street. It's also where our company is located.

WOMAN: Good, that's pretty close to our house. Let me see... Do you have soccer classes? He is a big fan of soccer and dreams to be a football player in the future.

MAN: Sure. We have exceptional soccer pitches available for our membership. Our sport-specific staff will ensure that your young athlete will gain some new skills and improve his physical fitness (*Q3*) through the soccer class.

WOMAN: Sounds great. Do we need to bring anything? A helmet, knee pads, soccer ball...

MAN: No. No need to bring any equipment, and the ball (*Q4*) will be provided by us. Just come. But it will be really hot in June, so I guess your son could wear a hat (*Q5*) to protect himself from the searing sun.

WOMAN: OK, I'll remind him of that.

WOMAN: I noticed that you have several different groups. Which group should my son join?

MAN: We place campers into groups based on age and ability. How old is your son, and has he had professional training?

WOMAN: He is currently ten years old and has never received training before.

MAN: Then the senior group will be a perfect fit for him. It's for older kids and also for beginner to intermediate-level players.

WOMAN:　Are there any other activities in this group?

MAN:　We've planned a talk, and the topic is about how to balance your diet (*Q6*), which I believe is worth listening to.

WOMAN:　I strongly recommend you to also add some lectures about injuries. You know, boys are always being naughty and getting hurt.

MAN:　Haha, alright. We'll consider your suggestion carefully. Perhaps you'll get to hear a lecture on it next time.

WOMAN:　I'm looking forward to it.

MAN:　After the class, there are several activities for fun as well. For example, the talent show, which allows their personality to shine. And we've noticed that many kids are passionate about competition (*Q7*), so we've decided to organize one to boost their enthusiasm for sports and teach them how to collaborate with teammates.

WOMAN:　Wow, that sounds interesting. My son would love it. Oh, I forgot to ask about the starting time of these activities. When should we arrive there?

MAN:　The time for the talent show has not been decided yet, but the competition will be held on June 15th, starting at 4:30p.m. (*Q8*). But it's better to arrive there 20 minutes early. The coach will help the kids do some warm-up exercises to prevent muscle strain.

WOMAN:　I see. We'll arrive there on time. Does my son need to be present when I sign up for him? I plan to do that on Monday, but I think he will be at school at that time.

MAN:　No worries. He doesn't need to be there in person. A parent can do the registration. When you get there, you should contact Emma Costa.

WOMAN:　Sorry, Emma...

MAN:　Costa. C-O-S-T-A (*Q9*). Also, you can call her on her phone. Her number is zero four one nine, five four three, double two eight (*Q10*).

WOMAN:　Okay. Thank you very much.

MAN:　You're welcome.

Part 2

WOMAN: Hello, welcome to our channel. Today we have invited James here to give us a preview of some of the upcoming Queensland Festival events. Hi, James.

MAN: Hello, everyone. I'm really excited to be here. I would like to share some of the latest news about the coming festival activities. As is shown on our website, you will not be charged for admission on weekends. But as you can imagine, it will be very crowded, so I strongly recommend you to visit here on Tuesday, unless you want to see a sea of people (*Q11*). No matter what day of the week it is, you can join some classes together with your kids, learning about geography, history, art and so on.

Also, we will organize an educational talk which aims at sharing some tips to improve the interaction between parents and children. Originally, it was only held on weekends, but later it became so popular that we changed its schedule, so now you can take part in the talk on any given afternoon (*Q12*).

Besides that, there will be a fantastic light show at 8:00p.m. every day. You shouldn't miss it. Oh, but I must remind you that the show will not be included in the festival entrance ticket, which means you must pay some extra money for it. You will get a pamphlet showing you the sites of where you can buy tickets to the show. Obviously, the sites in the city are closer to most of you, but some of you will suffer from the severe traffic congestion, so it will take you almost the same amount of time to get to the library in the suburbs. Tickets there are cheaper than if you buy them in the city because you'll get an 80% discount (*Q13*).

There are also many hot spots for you to visit – for example, the Mount Crosby Castle. When you walk in the castle, you will see a fascinating garden where you can walk around. It's a perfect place for those who love history because the castle is of great historical importance. Queensland was known by Europeans before the 1600s. But it was not until 1606 that the Dutch explorer Willem Jansz first landed on the Cape York Peninsula, and the castle was built right on his landing site (*Q14*). I suppose the castle is also a good choice for those interested in architecture since it typifies some of the early Queensland architectural style.

Next is one of our most popular events – the Food Festival. You may notice that the camping tent in that area is much bigger than last year's, and a variety of activities will be carried out there. During the event, a popular singer who has won many national awards will meet us and share his new songs (*Q15*). After these activities, our local chefs will serve you many specialties for your enjoyment.

Test 6
录音文本

221

If you still have some spare time, why not visit the Workshops Rail Museum, which will also be open to the public during the festival. In the exhibition, you can learn how to identify steam locomotives using the Queensland Railway classification system. Although you won't be able to see how the steam engines operate, you can enjoy meals with your family in the railway carriage after 6:00 p.m. (**Q16**) Near the carriage will be an exhibition of the old uniforms which display some of the local clothing stitched by hand. Even these days, you will possibly see some characters dressed in the full period costume.

If you plan to visit there with your family, the family ticket is good value for money. With the ticket stub, the staff will give you a colourful flag to wave (**Q17**). And the ticket also covers a visit to Brisbane Tramway Museum. There will be descriptions for each exhibit, but if you'd like to learn more details, you can hire our trained guide to give you more information, and that will cost you 6 pounds per hour. Some dolls, model cars and toy robots will be placed on the table in the museum just for decoration, so please remind your kids not to touch them. What your kids are allowed to take is the book on the bookshelf, which introduces the development of trams and trolleybuses (**Q18**). Another fringe benefit of the family ticket is that with another 5 pounds, you can get a meal voucher and enjoy your meal in a train cabin with your family.

Every year, we will vote for the most popular annual event and we sincerely invite you to participate in the voting. All the migrants and travellers, not just the people living there, have the right to vote, regardless of your age (**Q19**). Hit your new message button, put our phone number in the "To:" field, and write your favourite activity. Everyone has one vote per day, but after midnight, you will get a chance to vote again (**Q20**). All the activities will end on Saturday night and the voting phone lines will close at midnight three days after that, so please make full use of all your votes!

Again, thank you for listening to our channel and we are really looking forward to meeting you.

Part 3

MAN:　　Hi, Fiona. Have you read the journal I sent you about the excavation of the early Sarmatian burial ground near the village of Prokhorovka?

WOMAN:　Yeah, it's really amazing. The news said three burials were discovered with various grave goods. These included a silver bowl decorated with some gold plating. And what struck me most was that even though some archaeologists were not at the scene, they were as excited as if they had found the burial themselves (**Q21**).

MAN:　　Ha-ha, they do have a great passion for archaeology. Also, thanks to the volunteers, they did a very good job of preserving the archaeological site. How about writing something about this discovery in our archaeology final essay?

WOMAN:　Good idea. It is very impressive, after all.

WOMAN:　Do you have any idea where the silver bowl come from? Is it possible that it belonged to the church?

MAN:　　No, I don't think so. At that time, the church placed a unique pattern on everything it owned. But you can't find the special pattern on this bowl.

WOMAN:　You're right. I think it's more likely to be a rich man's burial object (**Q22**).

MAN:　　Very likely, because a skeleton of a man was discovered accompanying it (**Q22**).

WOMAN:　Where are the objects now? I mean, I heard that they were first spotted by a local resident, so who has the ownership of these objects, the museum or the local resident?

MAN:　　All of these discoveries have been sent to the local museum. They are precious cultural relics and will be well-preserved there.

WOMAN:　Great. So going back to our essay, I think we already have enough material for it. Shall we try to finish it this afternoon?

MAN:　　Well, I have to say that you're being too ambitious. We are far from writing up the essay because there are tons of other things to do, like, first, finding some images and videos related to the excavation and sorting them out, and then preparing the slides, deciding the research method... (**Q23**)

WOMAN:　Oh, you're right. How about completing the first step this afternoon? (**Q23**)

MAN:　　That sounds reasonable (**Q23**).

WOMAN:　But we have to work fast to meet the final deadline, right?

MAN:　　Actually, I don't think we need to be in a hurry. As long as we have organized the structure, catching up on the essay won't be a problem. But the problem is that our tutor has given us too much material about archaeology, so that might be challenging for us to pick out what we really need and try to condense it (**Q24**).

WOMAN:　What's the word limit?

MAN: She told us to write within 2000 words. That's my main concern now (**Q24**).

WOMAN: Well, I believe I can handle that. However, I'm a little worried about the presentation. You know, speaking in public has always been one of my nightmares. And... although I have faith in our topic, which is novel and up-to-date(**Q25**), I'm afraid that my writing style is not consistent with the academic writing style.

MAN: Never mind that. We can revise it together after finishing the first draft.

WOMAN: Thanks, Harry.

....

WOMAN: Have you read any of the literature recommended by our tutor?

MAN: Yes. The first book I read was *Archaeological Excavations in Greece*, which was too long for me to finish it all. I just noted the main idea of each chapter.

WOMAN: Yeah, it contains lots of details, such as the description of the excavation site and a list of all the people involved, which are pretty useful. But I can't find the place where the event occurred in Chapter Two. Then I browsed the internet to search for the place, and found that it actually doesn't exist (**Q26**).

MAN: Oh, the author must have made a mistake about it.

WOMAN: And I also read the book *Discovering Our Past*. It introduces lots of background information about archaeological excavations, explaining the definitions of some important terms in this field (**Q27**). If you are new to archaeology, it would be a great reference.

MAN: It sounds that it's suitable for beginners. To be honest, I haven't read that book yet. But I've read another one called *Reading Stratigraphy*.

WOMAN: I've read it, too. What impressed me most about the book is that it has a very long bibliography (**Q28**).

MAN: About four or five pages, right?

WOMAN: Five pages. I must admit that the bibliography inspired me to analyse things from different angles. Oh, and I highly recommend the book *Techniques of Archaeological Excavations*. I found it boring and dull at first. But later on, I indulged in the book and just couldn't put it down (**Q29**).

MAN: I felt the same way about it, actually. And I think you would like this book, too–*Roman Remained in Britain*. It's a well-organized book with a clear structure. However, one problem is that, if I recall correctly, the book doesn't mention anything about the silver bowl, which I think is an essential part in our essay (**Q30**).

WOMAN: I agree. We can't finish it without mentioning the bowl. Well, the next thing...(faded)

Part 4

Good morning, today I'm going to give a short presentation, summarizing my research project about rural life in our local area in the early thirteenth century. I chose to investigate this period because it was a time of great change and interest where many aspects of life—economic, social and technological were changing. I derived my information from a variety of sources—most of it from archives held in the museum (*Q31*) and some very valuable information from the Internet. I was surprised how many good websites there were on this topic. Finally, quite later on in my research, I contacted the city library. The librarians there helped me track down a map (*Q32*) which proved extremely informative for the project.

Now, at this time, nine-tenths of the population were working the land on small farms. An average household farmed between ten and thirty acres of land and most homes had deep ditches around them which were dug not for drainage, but in order to provide protection (*Q33*). As is often the case in periods of significant change and mobility, there was considerable unrest in the region. There are indications that in this area the main purchases for wealthier households were pottery for cooking purposes and also spices, which obviously had to be brought in from very far away, unlike herbs which they grew themselves. We are able to deduce this from the number of different kinds of shops (*Q34*) selling these types of products in settlements in the area.

Turning now to the crops, these were mainly cereals and legumes, peas and beans. These latter were extensively grown because they fertilized (*Q35*) the land and made anything planted after them grow well. The science behind this, the fact that legumes add nutrients by converting atmospheric nitrogen, was not known until the late nineteenth century. People simply found out these properties by trial and error. Another feature of farming at that time was the fact that because they weren't changed by chemicals and genetic modification, many crops had their own built-in protection. Serial seats, for example, were covered in a thick case of chaff which meant they were protected against diseases such as rust and also against assaults by birds (*Q36*).

Now I'm going to look at things which are undergoing change at this time. Firstly, one farming practice which was being introduced at this time was crop mixing. This was planting two or more crops at the same time on the same piece of land, for example, planting wheat and rye together. This can only be done in conditions where crops are harvested slowly by hand rather than machinery, which of course was the case at this time because that way people were able to harvest selectively. It means that if the weather is unsuitable for one crop, it is usually better for the other. This way, a reasonable harvest is ensured (*Q37*). Another innovation in the local area at this time was the introduction of the heavy plough, which was replacing the scratch plough. The heavy plough dug much deeper and enabled seeds to be planted securely and therefore to grow better. This brought long lasting changes to farming. Because heavy ploughs were less maneuverable, the draft animals, usually oxen at this time, but sometimes heavy horses, couldn't change direction easily. So it was better to change from short to very long thin fields (**Q38**). This gradually happened in our area at this time.

Now as many of you know our area is famous for its high winds and windmills of all shapes and sizes that had been used for a wide variety of purposes for a long time well before the thirteenth century. What was introduced at this time was fixing the sails onto a post which could easily be maneuvered to put the sails in the position to make the most of the available wind (**Q39**). Finally, I'd like to mention a particularly interesting change which was largely social rather than technological. This was the fact that at this time, poorer farmers with small holdings were actually beginning to produce higher yields from their land than their rich lords and masters. Both groups knew of good new practices of exhaustive weeding and more intensive planting. But this was highly labor intensive. This suited the poor smallholders because they had family members to draw on to do the work (**Q40**). The lords had to hire in such labor so they seldom bothered. Those the gap between rich and poor gradually began to narrow.

04

Section 4

参考答案

Test 1

	Part 1		Part 3
1	Club	21	A
2	male	22	B
3	drive	23	C
4	Tuesday	24	C
5	August/ two weeks	25&26 (in either order)	A B
6	dinner		
7	25/twenty-five	27	B
8	16/sixteen	28	D
9	modern plays	29	A
10	hospital(s)	30	C
	Part 2		Part 4
11	B	31	B
12	A	32	A
13	A	33	I
14	C	34	F
15	cards	35	B
16	spare	36	E
17	car(s)	37	D
18	colour/ color	38	C
19	printer	39	killer whales
20	ink	40	decline

Test 2

	Part 1		Part 3
1	nurse	21	A
2	0407686121	22	B
3	headaches	23	C
4	colds	24	B
5	seafood	25	A
6	eyes	26	B
7	30/thirty	27	B
8	park	28	D
9	yoga	29	A
10	sports centre/ sports center	30	E
	Part 2		Part 4
11	29.50/29.5	31	smooth
12	58/fifty eight	32	protection
13	passport	33	half
14	National Holidays	34	still / stagnant
15	Beanham	35	salt
16	PL239PU	36	mud
17	directions	37	smell
18	car parking	38	pump
19	restaurant	39	pest
20	website	40	antibiotic

参考答案

Test 3

Part 1		Part 3	
1	11 years	21-23	
2	book	(in either	B C G
3	babies	order)	
4	bridges	24	environmental
5	football	25	petrol
6	drama	26	supply
7	games	27	batteries
8	circus	28	expensive
9	hat	29	store
10	016 1962 3388	30	engines
Part 2		Part 4	
11	B	31	B
12	A	32	A
13	C	33	B
14	A	34	E
15	B	35	B
16	C	36	C
17	A	37	methods
18	B	38	outdoors
19	C	39	light
20	B	40	essays

Test 4

Part 1		Part 3	
1	8.25	21	B
2	water	22	A
3	walk	23	B
4	woods	24	C
5	10/10:00	25	C
6	boots	26	A
7	cousin	27	D
8	restaurant	28	F
9	pay	29	B
10	stamps	30	E
Part 2		Part 4	
11	A	31	furniture
12	A	32	service
13	A	33	insurance
14	B	34	schools
15	C	35	jobs
16	D	36	campus
17	E	37	traffic
18	A	38	cycling
19	G	39	retail
20	F	40	office

参考答案

Test 5

	Part 1		Part 3
1	7:45	21	C
2	write	22	B
3	140	23	B
4	56	24	C
5	certificate	25	B
6	knife	26	A
7	neck	27&28	
8	towel	(in either order)	B E
9	Lawnton	29&30	
10	mirror	(in either order)	C E
	Part 2		Part 4
11	B	31	temperature
12	A	32	movement
13	A	33	roots
14	B	34	bones
15	A	35	feathers
16	G	36	pollution
17	D	37	space
18	F	38	sharks
19	E	39	chicks
20	C	40	diversity

Test 6

	Part 1		Part 3
1	swimming	21	B
2	High	22	B
3	fitness	23	B
4	ball	24	A
5	hat	25	A
6	diet	26	D
7	competition	27	C
8	4:30 p.m.	28	G
9	Costa	29	A
10	0419543228	30	E
	Part 2		Part 4
11	B	31	museum
12	C	32	map
13	A	33	protection
14	C	34	shops
15	B	35	fertilized
16	C	36	birds
17&18		37	B
(in either order)	B E	38	C
19&20		39	B
(in either order)	A D	40	C